Not just any man

A
PRACTICAL GUIDE
TO FINDING
MR. RIGHT

JENNIFER LOGAN

WORD PUBLISHING
Dallas · London · Sydney · Singapore

NOT JUST ANY MAN:
A PRACTICAL GUIDE TO FINDING MR. RIGHT

Scripture quotations used in this book are from The Holy Bible, New
International Version (NIV). Copyright © 1973, 1978, 1984
International Bible Society.

Library of Congress Cataloging-in-Publication Data

Logan, Jennifer, 1953-
    Not just any man : a practical guide to finding Mr. Right /
Jennifer Logan.
        p.   cm.
    ISBN 0-8499-0662-8
    1. Mate selection—United States.   2. Mate selection—Religious
aspects—Christianity.   3. Single women—United States.   I. Title.
HQ801.L595   1989
646.7'7—dc19   88-32256
                                                          CIP

Printed in the United States of America

9 8 0 1 2 3 9   AGF   9 8 7 6 5 4 3 2 1

To
the men and women
who have found each other
by using these principles.

Thank you for sharing your insights
with others.

CONTENTS

Confessions
of a
Matchmaker

Twelve years ago I was attending a party given by some friends from church when a handsome man walked up, introduced himself, and talked to me briefly. Before he moved on to mingle with other guests, he asked if I would like to go to dinner with him the following week. I said, "I'd love to," and the rest is history. After dating for a year, we were married. We now have two wonderful children, are both involved in stimulating careers, and are more in love than we have ever been before.

Over the years, as I have been enjoying my life, I've wished the same happiness for my single friends and co-workers. Some have even come to me and asked how to find a man like my husband—a man who shares the same values, who is a terrific husband and father, and who is also a fun person to be around. The fact is, I think my husband, Bob, is one in a million. But I also know that there are other great guys out there who are looking for women who want the same things out of life that they do. But how in the world do you find each other?

In this crazy world in which we live, it's not easy to find guys who come close to your ideal of what a good date should be—let alone what a good husband should be. The problem is so prevalent that it has become a favorite topic of cartoonists and has spawned at least one line of greeting cards. But I don't have to convince you of the problem. My single friends have told me story after story about dating disasters. You could probably contribute a few yourself.

So what's a woman to do? Get busy!

Today, the burden of finding an eligible man rests primarily on the shoulders of eligible women. Yet as I've talked to dozens of single men and women over the years, I've been shocked at how uninformed they are about how to find each other. Many of the women think that romance novels reflect real-life scenarios—a wonderful man seems to appear out of nowhere, recognizes that the woman has hidden qualities that have gone undiscovered by other men, and then the two of them fall madly in love, marry, and move into a mansion. No wonder so many single women are depressed when they look at the three unmarried men in their church week after week, wondering if one of them could possibly be a romantic hero in disguise.

You may be wondering about my story. Wasn't that pure chance? Didn't Bob just happen to appear at the party, and didn't he just happen to ask me to dinner and then fall madly in love and carry me off to happily-ever-after-land? Not quite. Without my actively working at it, we never would have met. If I hadn't used specific techniques, he never would have really noticed me. And even though he asked me to dinner, I had already let him know that I was interested in spending time with him. When I recently confessed all of this to Bob, he was shocked. "I never had a chance, did I?" he laughed. But he isn't complaining, and neither am I.

To be honest, I wasn't all that aware of the strategies I used to find Bob. I grew up in a time and culture where techniques of flirtation were learned along with table manners. I was encouraged to cater to men's interests, to make them feel good about themselves, to be the kind of woman men wanted to be around. If I sound like a prehistoric woman living in a post-women's-liberation culture, you may be right. I was surprised to find that women from different backgrounds hadn't learned the same "techniques" I had. And I was amazed to see women younger than I—the products of a "liberated" world—unaware of some of the social graces I had learned as simple good manners.

But as I progressed in my career and began to give business advice to younger women, I found many of them would confess unhappiness with their personal lives. When I saw the way some of them related to men, I began to see why. They seemed to lack insight into the male ego. Some of them wanted to make every man aware of the inequities women encounter. Others simply seemed unaware of the age-old ways men and women let each other know that they are attracted to one another.

From the men I knew, I heard complaints about unapproachable women, concerns about career-oriented women, and some not-so-subtle cries for attention. Caught in the conflicting messages of the modern world, many men seemed confused and lonely. They were afraid of being "shot down," of being considered chauvinists if they wanted to marry someone who valued motherhood, of finding that a woman was so independent that she didn't need a man at all.

For years I listened to the two sides of this issue and finally I couldn't stand it anymore. I began to offer advice. I suggested ways that a single young woman in my office could let a man know she was interested. It worked! They were married a year later. I helped another woman meet men when she moved to a new town. Within six months she was dating several men—and her roommates began to come to me for similar advice. When a bright, beautiful business associate admitted that she had given up on marriage altogether, I suggested some specific techniques that she might want to use with the man she had admired from afar. Although she was a brilliant professional, she had never figured out how to relate to this man until we came up with a strategy. I am sure she will be married to her Mr. Right by the time this book is in your hands.

Women who had once considered my ideas about men and dating to be old-fashioned quietly began to confess an interest in some of my suggestions. Sometimes they laughed at my advice. But every woman who tried the methods discussed in this book found success.

As a journalist, I was intrigued with men's views of the current state of dating and relating, so I began an informal research project. I asked men what they really wanted in a relationship, what made them feel good about themselves, where they met women, and just about every other question I had heard women asking. They were honest with me, perhaps more honest than they had been with the single women they knew; after all, I'm an old married woman. When I shared some of their advice with my single women friends, light bulbs seemed to go on. "So that's why . . ." was a common reaction to the men's comments.

Over the years, as I've helped single men and women find each other, I've been called a matchmaker. I'm happy to wear that label because to me it means I've played some small role in bringing happiness to other people's lives. Mostly I've listened to men and women talk about their likes and dislikes, beliefs, and misconceptions. I've helped some men gain the courage to ask women out, but mostly I've advised women because they seem to bear the heavier burden in the dating game.

Why does the burden rest on women? First of all, I think women know what they want more than men do. Furthermore, because of their biological clock, women have only a limited number of years available to meet, marry, and have children. Ask a thirty-year-old single man if he wants to get married and he may say, "Eventually." Time is not a serious factor for him. I know single men in their fifties who are only now starting to settle down and seriously consider marriage. And why should they be concerned? Every year there are more women from which to choose. And chances are the younger the woman, the more she will look up to him and think him wise and experienced. Studies show that when men remarry, they tend to marry a woman who is four to seven years younger than they are. But every passing year means fewer options for women.

This book is a guide for the woman who is willing to admit that she wants to be married to a wonderful man and is ready to do some work to make it happen. Not only does it contain practical suggestions that have worked for me and for other women, but it also includes men's perspectives on a variety of topics, with frank discussions on everything from flirting to sex. Some of these topics are discussed from the general perspective of the Christian woman. Others are best illustrated by the real-life stories of men and women I know. In most cases, I have changed the circumstances slightly to protect the privacy of these individuals. And in every case, I have used different names.

The principles here are not only meant to "catch" a man, but they can also help you keep him and have a wonderful life together. For example, flirting is as essential to the marriage relationship as it is to attracting a man in the first place. So are most of the other aspects of relationships you will learn about in the chapters to come. The investment you make in the process of finding your Mr. Right will be a lasting benefit to you and your future husband.

One final confession: Jennifer Logan is not my real name, and my husband's name isn't Bob. Neither of us is willing to expose the intimate details of our courtship to the world. Nor are we willing to put our single friends at risk of embarrassment. We don't think it's that important that you know who we are, beyond the fact that we truly are happily married. What we really want is for you to have a real-life romance that leads to a marriage that is as happy and fulfilling as ours.

One word of advice before you begin your adventure in romance: be willing to give every method in this book a try. If you really want to be married and are diligent in following these principles, you will meet many men in the months to come. You will begin dating those who interest you. And in one year from today, you should have narrowed down the prospects in your search for Mr. Right. Believe me, the techniques in this book will work if you try them. So be prepared for your social life to change dramatically. And be sure to send me an invitation to your wedding!

cathy®

by Cathy Guisewite

CHAPTER ONE

Lonely Hearts

Oㅤne of my favorite cartoons is "Cathy." I think the plights of this single woman are so funny because they hit so close to the truth. In cartoon after cartoon, Cathy is shown looking for Mr. Right. But instead she finds only "Mr. Maybe's." Cathy is not the only one facing this situation.

Look around at the people you know. Doesn't it seem like there are lots of attractive, together, interesting single women? And doesn't it seem that there are very few attractive, together, interesting single men? If you think that it's just you, or just the people you know, or just the area in which you live, look again. The fact is that if you are a single woman looking for a relatively nice, attractive, together, interesting man, the odds are against you.

For many women, this hunch was confirmed by a 1986 study called "Marriage Patterns in the U.S." According to the report, white, college-educated women who are single at age thirty have only a 20 percent chance of marrying. By age thirty-five, the odds drop to five percent. Because men tend to marry younger women, the men who are your age will begin dating younger and younger women as they leave college and begin their careers. Many won't be ready to settle down until they are nearing thirty—but they will probably marry a woman who is in her early twenties. Each year you delay marriage, there are fewer men in your "pool" of prospects.

Because of these simple demographic trends, there's never been a more difficult time to follow the seemingly natural path toward love and marriage. In fact, in the world in which we live, there's nothing at all natural or easy about relatively compatible men and women finding each other. And if you consider the additional preferences of shared values, lifestyle, and goals, the odds are *heavily* against you.

So what's a woman to do? Many single women delude themselves into thinking the problem isn't serious. They waste valuable months and years believing that somehow circumstances will change and their life will become a whirl of activity leading to Mr. Right.

Other women passively submit to the situation, sinking into depression and pinning their hopes on a fantasy-land idea of the romantic hero who strolls into a woman's life and plucks her out of her boredom.

Neither of these approaches brings you any closer to a real-life romance. The only way things will change in your life is for you to face the facts and then pursue a plan of action to meet and marry the man of your dreams.

FACE THE FACTS

None of us likes to hear bad news. But the fact is—times are tough for single women. And the simple fact that there are more women than men is only a small part of the problem. An even greater obstacle that is keeping marriage-able men and women apart is the belief in three myths that have gained popularity in recent years—the myth of independence, the myth of equality, and the myth of attraction. Let's take a closer look at each one and see how belief in these myths may be blocking your path to Mr. Right.

The Myth of Independence. Women today are more independent than they have ever been. They pursue studies that lead to careers. Instead of marrying after high school or college, as their mothers or grandmothers did, today's women head straight for the working world.

Once upon a time, not too many years ago, women were encouraged to be *dependent*—or to at least appear as if they were. They learned to look for someone to take care of them, to carefully avoid studies other than home economics or education, and to find a way to lead a boyfriend to commitment before graduation.

Of course, many a dependent woman married a less than compatible guy, lost her own identity, and was unprepared to care for herself if anything happened to him. She is a figure who was often held up during the last decade as a victim of society. It's true that there are many displaced homemakers who wish they had learned to fend for themselves earlier in life. But there are far more "independent" women who have let their fear of dependence in any form keep them from establishing healthy relationships.

FACT: Dependence is part of every relationship.

Whether it's a friendship with another woman or a business relationship with a boss or co-worker, there is an element of dependence whenever we relate meaningfully and over time to another human being. To run from that is to undermine the ability to connect and interact and, ultimately, to love.

Today's world is full of lonely, unloved, *independent* people. Independence is exalted as a virtue to the point that many people (and especially single women) think they should take great pride in being independent. Yet there is no greater virtue in being independent than there is in being dependent.

If you are a woman who has taken up the independence battle cry, learn to see that dependence can be healthy. Think about all of the people you *do* depend on—your parents, your friends, the people at work—and what benefits you derive from those relationships. If you have been hurt by someone you have depended on, try to forgive that person and move on. Remember that the alternative to being dependent and risking hurt is to be totally independent and have no relationships at all.

You may be saying to yourself, "Surely there are men who are looking for independent women." After interviewing dozens of single and married men, I have concluded that this is more a matter of fantasy than reality.

> FACT: Men want women to need them.

Like many concepts, independence is one that men believe they should endorse, but under the surface, their feelings are ambivalent. Yes, they want a woman who doesn't cling to or smother them; but at the same time, they do want what they would view as "healthy dependence" or what might be defined as the ability to make a man *feel* needed.

Everyone needs to be needed. And the basic fact is that men and women do need each other desperately. It is true biologically, psychologically, and societally. Just because a woman doesn't depend on a man for income doesn't mean she will never need a man.

Men are confused by the talk about independence. It cuts to the very core of their ego and self-image. A man tends to feel put down when he is not needed. He tends to think that he must not be strong enough or successful enough or smart enough to warrant a woman's full attention. I'm convinced, however, that many times men and women are describing a similar ideal relationship even though men may add the caveat "I don't want a woman who is too independent" and women may say "I want to have my own identity in some way." If a negotiator could sit down and spell out the exact assumptions, I believe most men and women could comfortably compromise. But a word like *independence* is loaded with different meanings, depending on who says and hears it.

If you are a woman who verbally or nonverbally tells men you don't need them, with the mistaken idea that you are being attractively independent, you better think again. It is all right to present a bit of a challenge to a man. But only the men with the strongest egos can deal with a woman who openly says "I don't need you." To most men the message is one of personal rejection.

So why worry? Why should women be concerned about the fragile male ego? If you are interested in marriage, it is critical that you dispel the notion that you shouldn't be too concerned about men's perceptions.

The Myth of Equality. We have all heard that men and women have equal rights to jobs, pay, and advancement. We have seen laws enacted aimed at providing more equal treatment of men and women. But don't be fooled. When it comes to the real world of relationships, men and women are not equal.

FACT: Men have more options.

The biological clock does not tick at the same rate for men and women. For one thing, men are not as limited in their opportunities to have children. Generally a woman has until her mid- to late-thirties to find a man and have children. However, some men don't even consider marriage until they are well into middle age.

Furthermore, as I mentioned earlier, the older a man gets, the more women he has from which to choose. And men tend to like younger women because younger women make less demands on them and need them more. Young women think that older men are wise and sophisticated compared to younger men. But the older a woman is, the fewer men she has available. Although some men like older women, it is more of an exception than a rule. And many women have a tough time dating men more than a year or two younger than themselves.

> FACT: Most men are not nearly as liberated as women think they are.

The modern man believes that he is supposed to embrace a certain philosophy or he will be characterized as a male chauvinist pig. The fact is that most men are not nearly as modern as they seem.

When I interviewed men, they were quick to support women's rights and opportunities. But when I asked more specific follow-up questions, it became clear that many modern men have very traditional ideas of how their relationships will actually transpire. Many men affirmed a woman's career, but admitted that they had reservations about her juggling both career and family.

One man said he expected to marry a career woman, but "not someone who would want to work while raising a family." Another man affirmed that he thought a woman should work, but said, "I wouldn't want to marry someone who is as caught up in her career as I am in mine."

Few men thought they'd feel comfortable marrying a woman who was more successful than themselves. And most still thought it was the woman's job to take care of the home and raise children.

Perhaps these views make you frustrated or angry. But remember, these are simply the facts. The average guy you know is probably neither the modern liberated man you hope he is nor the male chauvinist you fear he is. More than likely he is somewhere in between and simply confused by the talk about modern relationships and his own definite preferences for the more traditional roles.

The Myth of Attraction. We live in a world that places incredible emphasis on physical attractiveness. From the advertisers' point of view it makes perfect sense: the average person feels insecure in some way about his or her looks; therefore, emphasize the problems and sell solutions.

But the average woman doesn't have an hourglass figure, and the typical guy doesn't look like Tom Cruise. What's more, physical attractiveness has very little to do with the success of a relationship.

FACT: Shared values are the basis of solid marriages.

Many women want a guy who shares their values, outlook on life, and commitment to family; but instead of concentrating on these qualities, they often spend their time focusing on the way he dresses, the color of his hair, and the car he drives.

It used to be that single people met each other primarily through their families, friends, or churches, and developed relationships only after they had established the fact that they generally shared beliefs and values. Today women often leave their families to go to college and never return. They meet men through work, school, or happenstance and rely on physical attraction to narrow down their prospects. Too late, many women have discovered that physical attraction often follows friendship and commitment to the same principles. But beginning a relationship based on attraction often leads to disillusionment.

FACT: It is easier to find a man who attracts you than one who shares your value system.

If you are a woman who knows what she believes and is committed to her faith and values, you will have a difficult time meeting men. Fifty years ago the chances were great that many of your neighbors would have shared your basic beliefs. Even twenty years ago the basic Judeo-Christian values still guided most peoples' lives. In today's world, however, many people do not even know what they value. Finding men who value commitment, family, and marriage is not easy. Finding men who have these values and also share your religious faith is quite rare.

That's why it makes the most sense to start out looking for men who share your faith and values and *then* move on to compatibility and attraction. You are certain to be attracted to men who have very little in common with you. But after developing a friendship with a man who shares your values, you may be surprised at how attractive he becomes.

What about that "spark," that sense of head-over-heels attraction? Don't you need some amount of it in order to make a relationship last? Yes and no. Attraction is necessary, but it doesn't have to be dramatic, nor does it always happen right away.

To be honest, I wasn't overwhelmingly attracted to Bob when I first met him. I thought he was handsome and funny, but I had a mad crush on someone else at the time. Then I discovered that the dashing man I found so attractive was cruel and insensitive. Bob was kind and considerate; he was a friend for months before the romantic side of our relationship really blossomed. But when it did, it was based on mutual respect and shared values rather than a mad crush based on fantasy.

Many women concentrate so hard on looking for a guy to "knock their socks off" that they miss the opportunity to get to know a guy whose special qualities are less obvious. "I'm always attracted to the guy who is good looking, confident, and athletic," confessed a friend of mine. "Yet if he does ask me out, he tends to be arrogant and self-absorbed."

I watched this same friend ignore the interest of an average-looking guy who was "just a friend" for years. It wasn't until he gave up on her and married a friend of his younger sister that she realized her feelings of attraction toward him. "He never really 'wowed' me," she said. "But he made me laugh, we were comfortable together, and I think we would have had something to talk about when we were ninety." That kind of "comfortable" attraction has been ignored by moviemakers and television shows because it isn't dramatic. But that's what real-life marriages are made of—especially after the initial romance fades.

Susan and John are one of the most romantic couples I know. Even with five children, they seem to be on a perpetual date. When I asked Susan recently if it was love at first sight, she laughed. "Heavens, no. We were good friends in college and dated other people. After four years we realized that we had fallen in love with each other!"

If you are a single woman who wants to marry, you need to recognize the facts we've highlighted in this chapter. Maybe they don't represent an ideal world. But they do represent the reality in which you live.

Once you've understood the danger in believing these myths, you are ready to begin doing something about finding Mr. Right. Yes, I do believe he is out there. But you're going to have to work at finding him. But why *not* work at finding the most important person you will ever know? The search certainly deserves as much attention as your career or any other aspect of your life.

The game plan is first to learn more about yourself and how to relate to men. This new understanding of yourself will help you not only to find the man you want to marry, but in the process, you will also learn how to attract his attention, how to get him to ask you out, and how to continue to nurture the relationship.

It may be that the advice in this book will seem conservative to some. It is written specifically for the woman who is looking for a man who shares her values. For some women, that will mean a commitment to a conservative faith and lifestyle. These are the women who, I believe, have struggled the most in these changing times. Although they remain true to certain beliefs, many have been affected by the myths of modern thinking.

Many of the women who have met men by using the principles in this book had not dated for years. Some had nearly given up on finding anyone who shared their values. But one of the most common reactions to the principles in this book has been: "It was really simple once I figured out what I was doing wrong!"

Yes, it is simple. But that doesn't mean you won't have to work at developing your own strategy to fit your lifestyle, preferences, and situation.

As you begin your evaluation, make a promise to be honest with yourself and to believe that you're about to find Mr. Right. He's out there looking for you right now. Our challenge is to help him find you.

cathy®

by Cathy Guisewite

CHAPTER TWO

How Marriageable Are You?

But what about me?" you may be asking. Trends about men and society are helpful to understand, but what exactly does this have to do with my chances for finding Mr. Right?

And why is it that some very attractive women are sitting at home every Saturday night while their less attractive friends are dating someone? How is it that so many couples have found each other in the sea of people doing their own thing? Is there some way to know who will marry and who won't?

Of course, there is no way to predict who will marry or when they will say "I do." Libby Hanford, an attractive, outgoing, cheerful attorney, seemed to have many opportunities to marry, but didn't say "I do" until she was in her late thirties. Now known as Elizabeth Dole, she feels absolutely confident that waiting for the handsome senator from Kansas was exactly the way God had it planned.

Other women begin to get nervous about their prospects in their early twenties and wonder if they should "try" to fall in love with a man they know or someone who is interested in them. Instead of asking "How can I live without him?" they begin to ask questions like "Can I hope to do any better?"

If you are wondering where you fit in compared to other women, it's time to measure your personal marriageability.

THE MARRIAGEABILITY INDEX

Just what are your chances of getting married? And how hard must you work to overcome the natural or attitudinal or environmental obstacles to living happily ever after with the man of your dreams? The following quiz will give you an idea.

MARRIAGEABILITY QUIZ

Circle the appropriate answers to questions 1–15.

1. What is your age?

    A. Under 25

    B. 25–29

    C. 30–34

    D. 35–39

    E. 40 or over

2. Have you been married before?

    A. No

    B. Yes, but no children

    C. Yes, with children living at home

3. Have you dated anyone seriously in the last three years?

    A. Yes

    B. No

4. Have you dated in the last six months?

    A. No

B. 1 or 2 times

C. 3–5 times

D. 6–10 times

E. More than 10 times

5. How tall are you?

A. Under 5′

B. 5′–5′3″

C. 5′4″–5′6″

D. 5′7″–5′10″

E. Over 5′10″

6. What color is your hair?

A. Brown

B. Black

C. Blond

D. Red

E. Gray

7. How long is your hair?

A. Very short (less than 3″)

B. Fairly short (above chin length)

C. Medium (chin to shoulder length)

D. Long (shoulder length to mid back)

E. Very long (mid back or longer)

8. How would you characterize your weight?

A. Underweight by more than 10 lbs.

B. Slightly underweight

C. About right for my height

D. Overweight by less than 10 lbs.

E. Overweight by more than 10 lbs.

9. How many people work in your place of employment?

A. Less than 20

B. 20–100

C. 100–300

D. More than 300

10. How would you describe your personality?

A. Very outgoing

B. Fairly outgoing

C. Sometimes outgoing, sometimes shy

D. Somewhat shy

E. Very shy

11. How would you describe your relationship with your father?

A. Very close

B. Fairly close

C. Somewhat distant

D. Distant

E. Hostile

12. How do your dating relationships usually end?

A. He usually breaks it off

B. I usually break it off

C. About half have been my choice

    D. I don't know

    E. I haven't dated much

13. How long do your dating relationships usually last?

    A. One date

    B. Two to four dates

    C. A month or two

    D. Around six months

    E. More than a year

14. How do you think most people would describe you?

    A. Exceptionally attractive

    B. Attractive

    C. Pleasant looking

    D. Plain

    E. Unattractive

15. My style of dress during weekdays would be considered:

    A. Professional

    B. Feminine

    C. Casual

    D. Very Casual

    E. Artsy

Indicate your feelings by placing A, B, C, D, or E in front of each of the following statements:

    A. Agree strongly

    B. Somewhat agree

C. Somewhat disagree

D. Disagree strongly

E. Not sure

_____ 16. I believe in love at first sight.

_____ 17. The man I marry must share my religious beliefs.

_____ 18. The man I marry must not be previously divorced.

_____ 19. The man I marry should be handsome.

_____ 20. I get along well with most people.

_____ 21. I think I am a "good catch."

_____ 22. My career is very important to me.

_____ 23. I would like to marry soon.

_____ 24. It is easy for me to talk to men.

_____ 25. I dislike being alone.

SCORING

Now total your score by using the following numerical equivalents:

1. A. 0	2. A. 1	3. A. 0	4. A. 3
B. 1	B. 0	B. 3	B. 2
C. 2	C. 2		C. 0
D. 3			D. 0
E. 4			E. 2

5. A. 0	6. A. 2	7. A. 3	8. A. 3
B. 0	B. 1	B. 2	B. 1
C. 1	C. 0	C. 1	C. 0
D. 2	D. 2	D. 0	D. 2
E. 3	E. 3	E. 1	E. 3

9. A. 3	10. A. 1	11. A. 0	12. A. 3
B. 2	B. 0	B. 0	B. 2
C. 1	C. 0	C. 1	C. 0
D. 0	D. 2	D. 2	D. 1
	E. 3	E. 3	E. 1

13. A. 3	14. A. 1	15. A. 2	16. A. 3
B. 2	B. 0	B. 0	B. 2
C. 1	C. 0	C. 0	C. 0
D. 0	D. 1	D. 1	D. 0
E. 2	E. 2	E. 1	E. 0

17. A. 3	18. A. 3	19. A. 3	20. A. 0
B. 2	B. 2	B. 2	B. 0
C. 0	C. 0	C. 0	C. 2
D. 0	D. 0	D. 0	D. 3
E. 0	E. 0	E. 0	E. 1

21. A. 0	22. A. 3	23. A. 3	24. A. 0
B. 1	B. 2	B. 2	B. 1
C. 2	C. 1	C. 1	C. 2
D. 3	D. 0	D. 0	D. 3
E. 2	E. 0	E. 0	E. 2

25. A. 3
B. 2
C. 1
D. 2
E. 2   Total _____

What does your score mean? If it is more than 60, you have some environmental as well as attitudinal problems to overcome. Read on to discover specific ways to change areas in your life which will make you more marriageable.

If your score is 43–59, join the crowd. Most single women fall into this category. You have great potential, but you are making some mistakes in relating to men. Review your answers, then read on to learn more about the areas you can improve upon.

If your score is 29–42, you are doing very well in most areas, but a few blind spots must be keeping you and Mr. Right from finding each other. Be sure that you don't skip over the evaluation chapters in this book. You may be missing something that could change your social life dramatically.

If your score is 15–28, you are well on your way to finding Mr. Right. You don't need a great deal of help. Perhaps you just need some tips on meeting men. Or maybe you aren't as approachable as you think you are (see chapter 7).

If you scored under 15, you are "practically perfect in every way!" Are you being absolutely honest in your answers? Are you really perceived by other people as you perceive yourself?

OVERVIEW

For some additional insight into the scoring, here's a brief overview of the significance of your answers:

1. Your age is a given. The fact is that the older you are, the less chance you have of marrying. Obviously, that didn't stop Elizabeth and Robert Dole from finding one another. It needn't stop you, either.

2. Surprisingly, statistics show that a divorced woman

without children has a better chance of remarrying than a never married woman has of marrying for the first time.

3. If you have not dated anyone seriously (more than a date or two) in three years, you must not be meeting enough men or you may need help in learning how to relate to them. I can guarantee that the techniques in this book will help.

4. You are either too busy or not busy enough. Are you seen too often with the same guy if you aren't serious about him? Are you too picky? Most guys will be scared to ask out a woman who has turned down a friend. They fear rejection, too.

5. This is an area you cannot change. But the taller you are, the narrower the field of men who are either as tall as you or confident enough to ask out a taller woman. If you are tall, stand up straight and enjoy your special status as someone who can wear all the clothes your shorter friends would look lost in. If you're average height or shorter, be thankful. This is definitely an asset.

6. It's not just a myth. Gentlemen do prefer blonds. See chapter six for more details. If your hair is gray, read chapter 8 to see how this may work against you.

7. Yes, it's true. Most men like long hair, too. Again, see chapter six.

8. You won't lose points for a few pounds in either direction. But more than ten pounds over- or underweight means you have some work to do. Isn't it worth it to allow a man to see who you really are?

9. Since you spend more time at work than any place else, this is a natural place to meet men. If you work in a small office, don't panic. See chapter ten for some ideas.

10. You don't want to overwhelm a guy. But you don't want to underwhelm him either. Be careful of scaring him or making him carry the entire conversation.

11. One of the ways women learn to relate to men is based on the way they have related to their fathers. If you have had a good relationship with your father, chances are

you are comfortable with men. If the relationship has been strained or negative, you may need some professional counseling to help straighten out any unresolved anger. It's worth it—especially if you feel that patterns are developing in the way you view other men in your life.

12. Are you asking too much? Or are you asking too little? If you are the one who is always left behind, you need to work on self-confidence. See chapters five and six.

13. Beware of rushing a relationship or dragging along and being unwilling to commit to the future. See chapters five and twelve for more information about the phases of relationships.

14. Believe it or not, being too attractive can be a liability. Guys get scared away. If you fear that you are not attractive enough, read chapters five and six.

15. Being professional is good for your career, but bad for your social life. If you are too casual or artsy, you will attract a certain type of guy but may be written off by the average man.

16. You can either be overly romantic or overly realistic. You need balance.

17. It's not wrong to have a strong preference. It only limits your options.

18. Again, there's no right or wrong. But you will narrow the field.

19. Beware of falling into the attraction trap. See chapter four to learn more about what attributes you really value.

20. If you have some personality traits that turn off people, you will need to work on them. See chapter five for ideas on self-evaluation.

21. Being self-confident makes a big difference in how men perceive you. You don't need to be conceited to consider yourself a good catch. If you don't believe it, no one else will.

22. There is nothing wrong with caring about your career. But it will scare many guys away.

23. It's important to know what you want. But you can't seem desperate.

24. Maybe you're a natural conversationalist. But most of us have to learn this specialized art. See chapter nine for some very specific things to say to men—but watch out!

25. You don't want to seem clingy to men. But if you are too much of a loner, guys will be afraid that you don't need them.

Ready to improve that score? Then read on. Just be sure to have your date book sitting by the phone. You're going to need it.

CHAPTER THREE

Getting Started

Janet was late for work again. For the past several weeks, she'd been coming to work ten or fifteen minutes late every day. But Mondays were the worst. On this particular Monday, she walked in the door at 9:30, just as her boss came out of his office, threw some papers on her desk, and announced, "So nice of you to join us today."

When I passed her later that morning I asked her how she was doing. "Okay," she muttered unconvincingly.

"Want to have lunch?" I asked.

"Okay," she responded again.

Over lunch it became clear that Janet was barely okay. "I hate this job," she said. When I suggested that she look for something she'd enjoy more, she just shook her head. We talked for a while about what she liked and disliked about her work, but it seemed clear that Janet's problems went beyond job boredom.

I asked her if she'd had a nice weekend, and tears filled her eyes. "I haven't had a date for months," she said. "I went to a church party with a girlfriend, and the guys were either with a girl or were real losers. I left after half an hour."

"Janet, what do you really want?" I asked, trying to get at the root of her despair.

"I guess I want to be married," she said hesitantly. "I never really wanted a career. I just thought I'd work for a few years, then settle down and start a family. I'm scared that I'll spend the rest of my life alone, stuck with a job I hate and no one to share my life with."

Janet looked embarrassed by her confession. "I guess that's not a very modern outlook, is it?" she asked.

"I think it's fine," I said, trying to reassure her. "It's very important to know what you want out of life. There's nothing wrong with saying it. How else are you going to start doing something about it?"

Janet looked at me dubiously. "What do you mean 'doing something about it'?" she asked. "You make it sound like you can go out and just find the perfect guy on a shelf at the grocery store. I've been looking for years, but believe me, there aren't that many Prince Charmings around."

"But you know you want to get married, right?" I asked.

"Sure. But I don't want to marry just any guy," she said.

"Janet, a guy is not going to just fall out of the sky and into your life—especially a guy who has those special qualities you think are important," I said.

But Janet had grown up believing in the romantic notion that there would be one man for her and that he would sweep her off her feet and into a perfect marriage. Of course, as she grew older, she realized that some of the guys she dated looked like the perfect match, but turned out to be a frog disguised as a prince. When the guy she thought was "the one" left her for her best friend, she was devastated.

Janet's mother had always told her that God had a special man picked out for her. The longer Janet waited for him, the more she began to wonder if God was punishing her. The world seemed to be full of couples, but she continued to be alone.

Janet told me that she had never really thought about looking for a guy because she really believed that God would bring him into her life. When I asked her why she was so unhappy if she believed that would happen, she said, "I guess I'm just getting impatient with God."

We talked about the impact all this was having on Janet's faith and her self-image. Then I tried to give her my thoughts on the subject. "Janet, of course I believe that God can miraculously bring two people together. I know it has happened. But believing that God is in control is not the same thing as sitting back and waiting for him to do everything for you. You don't just sit back and wait for a job to come along, do you? You send out résumés, go on interviews and look at want ads. Why should you be passive about the most important relationship in your life?"

"But what about learning to accept my singleness?" Janet asked. "Some people say that I should learn to be content being single. But somehow I just can't do it."

"I don't agree with that philosophy," I told Janet bluntly. "Sure, there are people like Mother Teresa whose lives are special and who wouldn't be able to accomplish all they had to do in their lifetime if they were married. But I think they are the exception. Even the apostle Paul said, 'It is better to marry than to burn.' Just in that context he certainly seemed to underscore the importance and naturalness of marriage."

"All right," Janet said, somewhat defensively. "If you've got any great ideas about finding a man, I'd be glad to hear them."

I thought for a minute. Janet was so frustrated that I knew she needed to do something. She was beginning to think her life was hopeless when, in fact, she was a warm, wonderful person who just needed to be "discovered." Her attractiveness was hidden by her sad look and her depressive attitude.

It occurred to me that Janet's problem wasn't all that different from the ones the two of us faced each day in our marketing jobs. We often needed to take an unknown product and show the world how great it was, or take an underrated company and promote its hidden qualities.

I looked at Janet and began to smile. "You're going to think I'm crazy, but . . ." I said as I pulled a piece of paper out of my purse and wrote down some words. I showed the paper to Janet and she laughed. "You're serious, aren't you?" she asked.

"I am if you are," I challenged.

"It's worth a try," Janet said, and with that we formed a pact to help Janet find Mr. Right.

A STRATEGIC PLAN

The words I had written on the paper were "A Strategic Plan to Find a Husband for Janet." It was the same type of title we gave to marketing plans in our office. Janet and I agreed to meet for breakfast one day a week to specifically work on ways to reach her goal. I suggested that Janet bring to our breakfast meetings a looseleaf notebook, some paper to fit it, and dividers. Together we were going to create a marketing plan for Janet.

The strategy we developed over the weeks that followed includes the beginning steps that any woman can follow who would like to meet and marry the man of her dreams.

Start Fresh. It was Janet who discovered the first important principle in our strategy. Just the fact that she was willing to start fresh made a big difference in her attitude. It can work for you, too. Whether you are twenty-one or fifty-one, whether you're coming out of a serious relationship or haven't dated in years, *decide that you're ready to start fresh.* Ban the boyfriend blues from your life and begin to fill your mind with positive thoughts. Stop worrying about getting married. Worrying will only give you frown lines and health problems. Resolve instead to do something positive about finding a wonderful man to marry.

Say to yourself, "I will not give in to the temptation to

feel sorry for myself. I am a very special person about to be discovered by a very special man." And remember to smile. If you're walking down the street with a frown on your face or if you look depressed, Mr. Right may not recognize you. He may be afraid to approach you or mistakenly think you're not any fun.

Janet was beginning to be a more active participant in her life. Every morning when she woke up, she'd say to herself, "I am a very special person. Today may be the day I meet the man I will marry. I expect it to be a great day."

By focusing on her own depression and by spending time with friends who talked about the sad state of their own single lives, Janet had allowed herself to waste precious energy. Now she was beginning to fill her mind with positive thoughts and optimistic attitudes. Remember that you, too, are an active participant in your life. You don't have to wait for things to happen to you. As Dr. Robert Schuller, one of the world's greatest possibility thinkers, says, "If it's going to be, it's up to me."

Here are a few tips to get you started:

- Play uplifting music as you get dressed in the morning.

- Listen to tapes by Dr. Schuller, Norman Vincent Peale, Denis Waitley, Zig Ziglar, or other motivators on your way to work.

- Read motivational books and other positive literature.

- Consider the following quotes:

"If God be for us, who can be against us?" (Romans 8:31, NIV).

"A cheerful heart is good medicine, but a crushed spirit dries up the bones" (Proverbs 17:22, NIV).

"Finally, brothers, whatever is true, whatever is noble, whatever is right, whatever is pure, whatever is lovely, whatever is admirable—if anything is excellent or praiseworthy—think about such things" (Phillipians 4:8, NIV).

"Praise the Lord. Praise God in his sanctuary; praise him in his mighty heavens. Praise him for his acts of power; praise him for his surpassing greatness. . . . Let everything that has breath praise the Lord" (Psalm 150:1–2, 6, NIV).

Why all of the emphasis on attitude? Simply this: you may follow all of the guidelines in the next chapters, learn to dress correctly, understand men, and even find ways to meet them, but a negative attitude will undermine your best efforts.

You're in the Sales Business.   It may sound strange, but you are in the sales business as long as you are presenting yourself to the world as a woman who would like to marry a special man.

Most people who are in sales recognize the need to stay "up" even when they are turned down. They know the value of believing in themselves and quickly forgetting about defeats, while holding on to memories of accomplishments. They understand that worry about a sale doesn't do anything to sell their product.

You, too, must stay up, even if you don't get asked out by that special guy or if the only men you meet are a foot shorter and ten years younger than you (assuming that "disqualifies" them from your dating criteria).

Just imagine what might have happened if a new client —very handsome and single—had walked into our office the Monday that Janet rolled in at 9:30 looking disheveled, frustrated, and depressed? The first impression he would have had of Janet would have been so negative that it would have been nearly impossible for them to ever develop a relationship. As the shampoo commercial says, "You never get a second chance to make a first impression."

On a recent business trip I met a young woman who also seemed concerned about the fact that she wasn't dating anyone. We didn't have much time to talk, but I did notice that she seemed to look serious and depressed most of the time. Yet when she did smile, she had one of the loveliest smiles I had ever seen. During our brief visit, I was able to share a few tips on ways to meet men, but mostly I encouraged her to concentrate on being more positive and remembering to smile. A few weeks later she called and said, "This is Terry. I met you recently when you were in Chicago, and I just had to call to thank you for your advice. My life has really changed for the better!"

I felt as if I were hearing a modern version of "The Emperor's New Clothes." Terry hadn't really needed anything from me that she didn't have inside of herself already. But her willingness to believe in herself, to be more positive and optimistic, acted like a magnet in her life, attracting men to her. She was still the same person. But she looked like someone who had a great deal to be happy about. And both men and women always want to be around someone like that.

Roll Up Your Sleeves. I'm not going to try to fool you into thinking that you can meet the man of your dreams without some effort on your part. Meeting men is hard work—developing and sustaining a relationship involves a daily commitment.

Are you willing to make that investment? It will take time, effort, and courage. And it may very well mean learning new skills and abandoning comfortable patterns. Of course, I realize that some single women would rather complain about their miserable life than do something about it. So before reading any further, ask yourself the following questions:

cathy®

by Cathy Guisewite

- Am I willing to make finding the man of my dreams one of the top priorities in my life?

- Am I willing to consistently make the effort to find a man?

- Am I able to give up my dependence on passivity, depression, and pity?

If your answers are yes, then you are ready to jump into this exciting and challenging vocation of finding a husband. To take the plunge, here's what you can do:

1. *Spend fifteen minutes each and every day on the job of finding the man of your dreams.* Yes, it sounds simple. But Janet and Terry and other women have found that the fifteen minutes spent focusing on their attitude and approach made a very big difference in their lives.

2. Buy a looseleaf notebook in an attractive color, like the one I asked Janet to bring to our first session together. It should contain a supply of paper to fit the notebook, dividers—at least five—and tabs.

3. On the first page of your notebook write the following statement:

Starting today, _____(fill in date)_____, I am going to stop complaining about not finding the man of my dreams and start doing something about it. I will spend fifteen minutes every day on my plan.

Under your statement write the following:

Five minutes to be POSITIVE

Five minutes to feel PRETTY

Five minutes to be PRACTICAL

What do these three parts of the plan mean? Simple. Spend five minutes every morning putting yourself into the proper frame of mind. Start with a positive attitude.

Next, add five minutes to your grooming time to do something special for yourself. Add a pretty scarf to your outfit. Take a minute to look at yourself in a full length mirror, then make adjustments. Spray on perfume. Add a little special touch of makeup. Whatever you do, give yourself a little boost, as if you were meeting someone very special that day and wanted to look and feel extra pretty.

Finally, spend five minutes thinking about your day and the opportunities you will have to meet men. If you can't think of any at first, don't worry (see chapters nine and ten for ideas on places to meet men). Soon you'll come up with new ideas of your own. But for now, just mentally walk through your day and envision the places you go and the men you see. Who rides your bus to work? Who do you see at the office? Are there any men who you see regularly at the coffee shop where you have lunch? Begin to heighten your awareness of the men you see. In the next chapter, you'll begin to analyze these men with an eye toward your future.

So put a smile on your face, commit yourself to having a positive attitude, and embark on an adventure in learning more about yourself and more about the man you want to marry.

♥

CHAPTER FOUR

Write Your Own Romance Story

He was tall, dark, and handsome, and when he spoke her name, Nicole could feel her heart beating faster. She wondered if he could hear it. His piercing blue eyes crinkled in a smile as he reached out and guided her gently by the arm. 'I have a surprise for you,' he said. They walked together into the dining room where an elegant table was set for two. Candles were burning and there were fresh flowers on the table. 'I thought I'd cook a meal for the two of us,' he said. 'I hope you don't mind. I've wanted to have a quiet time just to get to know you.'

"'No, I don't mind at all,' she said, touched by his kindness and overwhelmed by his interest in her. He was everything she'd ever wanted in a man—handsome, considerate, masculine, and vibrant. She knew as he seated her at the table that this was the man she wanted to marry."

We've all read romantic stories in which the perfect man appears on the scene and immediately sweeps the heroine off her feet. It's all so simple, so sure, so . . . romantic. And yet from personal experience we realize that it rarely works that way. He seems like a nice guy, but there's something about his red hair that keeps you from being interested. You think he's the cutest guy at church, but he seems to think he's the most attractive guy in the world. You think he's funny, but he uses poor grammar and seems to have few aspirations in life.

MATCHING REALITY TO ROMANCE

When we read romance stories we never learn about those "human" features we all have—the things that some people don't notice and others find unbearably unattractive.

The other day I was talking to a friend who was recently widowed. Still quite young, she was beginning to date again after being out of circulation for nearly ten years. As my friend observed, "The second time around you're more realistic. You understand that finding someone to share your life with has less to do with being attracted to him than finding someone who doesn't drive you crazy in little ways. You have to know where you're willing to compromise."

Perhaps this view sounds unnecessarily cynical. But those of us who are happily married would be less than honest if we didn't admit to our spouse's shortcomings—as well as our own. A happy marriage consists of accommodation, acceptance, and sometimes learning to ignore the other person's humanness. And yet we all know that there are some things we absolutely could not live with.

At one point in my dating years, I was head-over-heels crazy about Scott. He was fun, attractive, witty, and sweet. He showed up on time for our first few dates. Then he began to be late. Every time we were scheduled to go somewhere, I was ready five minutes early and he was usually thirty minutes to an hour late. What's more, he never apologized for being late and acted irritated if I brought it up. Perhaps that doesn't sound like a big problem, but it was to me. I had been brought up to believe that keeping someone waiting is very rude. Scott's actions seemed irresponsible and inconsiderate to me. Over a short time, they undermined my interest in him.

No matter how wonderful Scott was, his consistent tardiness and lack of willingness to change made it impossible to continue our relationship. I'm not sure I would have listed "is always on time" on my list describing the man of my dreams. Yet, a man who didn't have my sense of timeliness would have driven me crazy.

Caroline, a good friend of mine, is pretty, sweet, and fun to be with. When she began to date Bill, he didn't seem to appreciate her, yet continued to ask her out. After a while, they became fairly serious, much to the amazement of most of Caroline's friends, who thought she could do much better than Bill. The relationship eventually deteriorated to the point where Bill was verbally abusive to Caroline in public and treated her cruelly. But she remained loyal to Bill for years.

When I asked Caroline if she ever grew frustrated with the relationship, she admitted that it wasn't ideal, but she didn't have any other men in her life and she thought Bill would "straighten out" after they married. Unfortunately, they eventually did marry, Bill became physically abusive, and the marriage ended in divorce.

Some single women, like Caroline, begin to be afraid that they will never marry and end up with a man who falls not only short of their dreams, but also short of acceptable behavior in a relationship. Other women look for any excuse to dismiss a guy without ever giving him a chance.

A critical element in finding a man to marry is understanding and developing realistic expectations. You need to believe in yourself enough to know that you are worthy of respect, kindness, and courtesy. But you must also join your romantic notions of the perfect man with reality. Although Janet and I had discussed the need to be wary about living vicariously through romance novels, in working through our strategy, we discovered that one of the best ways to move from the fantasy world to a workable plan for a real-life romance is to get in touch with your secret fantasies.

Thomas Wolfe said, "Is not this the true romantic feeling—not to desire to escape life, but to prevent life from escaping you?" Let's get in touch with those romantic feelings so we can get on with our plan.

NARROWING IT DOWN

When I asked Janet to describe her "perfect man" she giggled. "I guess I'm usually attracted to blond guys," she said. "But I'm not sure it really matters."

"Don't worry about the importance of any characteristic at this point," I suggested. "Just begin to develop a list of all the things you'd like in a man."

"He'd have to be a Christian," Janet began again. "And I prefer that he not be divorced."

"Would that rule him out?" I asked as I jotted down her description on a piece of paper from her notebook. "I guess it depends on the circumstances," she admitted. I wrote, *divorced?* on my paper in a column I labeled "dislikes." And *Christian* in a column I labeled "likes."

"Would he be tall?" I asked. Janet shrugged her shoulders. Since she was petite herself, she'd never really considered height an issue. I wrote *height* in a third column which I had labeled "not important."

"What about personality?" I asked.

Janet began ticking off preferences quickly: good sense of humor, but not too loud; thoughtful; kind to others; good with children; calm, but not too laid back; responsible. . . .

I was writing them down as she spoke. As she paused I asked her to tell me the characteristics she'd disliked in guys she had dated. "Tom had a good sense of humor, but he was too sarcastic. Jim was too possessive. Jerry was great, but the relationship never went anywhere because he didn't know what he wanted."

I added *sarcastic, possessive,* and *undirected* to my list of dislikes.

Janet spent the next week adding to the three lists. It was a fun exercise, and she found herself noticing guys on the bus, in the grocery store, and at church, and analyzing what she liked and disliked about them.

When we met again the following week she had revised the list several times. "I really like guys with dark hair just as well as blonds," she announced. "It's not a big deal, but I realized that I always thought I preferred fair-haired guys and didn't really look at guys with dark hair."

"I also realized that a guy's outlook is very important to me. I'd never thought about how important it is to me that a guy be upbeat and positive. It finally occurred to me when I really analyzed why I wasn't attracted to a guy at church who seems like a real 'catch.' His constant complaining is a real turn-off."

Janet admitted that her mother had always hoped she'd marry a doctor or a lawyer, but to Janet profession wasn't very important. She didn't care very much about money and status, so she didn't feel concerned about a man's line of work when dating. When I questioned her further on this point, she conceded that her mother's view had probably colored her thinking to some degree. She had avoided getting involved with a guy at church who was a struggling artist, since she knew her parents would think he was irresponsible. Yet Janet realized that this was her parents' prejudice, not her own, and began looking more closely at her assumptions about lifestyle and profession.

By the end of our third session together, Janet was feeling very positive about her prospects for marriage. She had started practicing positive thinking every day, and now she was developing more specific ideas about the man of her dreams. She realized that she was a great deal pickier than she thought she was.

I suggested that Janet concentrate on isolating five characteristics that were "must haves" in the man she would marry. When she narrowed the list down, she discovered an astounding fact: not one of the characteristics was a physical trait. Janet looked at me with surprise when I pointed that out.

"It's amazing how I spend so much time ruling out guys because they don't look quite right to me," she admitted. "And yet I guess looks don't really matter."

"Would you agree, then, that maybe you should go out with more guys and get to know them before you rule them out?" I asked as I turned to the section in her notebook we had marked "Strategy."

When Janet nodded, I wrote: 1. *Go out with more guys who are not immediately attractive to me.* It was our first active step toward finding a man for Janet. Although it seemed basic, Janet realized that she hadn't really considered her criteria for interest in guys before.

TAKE ANOTHER LOOK

One of my favorite questions to ask of married couples is how they met. From time to time I hear an amazing story of being stranded at a bus stop together or meeting on a ski lift. But the two most common answers I hear are: (1) We'd known each other for years and hadn't really been romantically interested; and (2) We thought we hated each other until we finally got to know one another. In both cases, the individuals knew each other but hadn't really noticed each other because they were busy looking for someone new and exciting.

Once you've discovered what you really want in a man, it's time to mentally review all of the men you know. Start a new section in your notebook and label it "Prospects." Begin to list guys you know under the following categories:

cathy®

by Cathy Guisewite

1. Men I know well. In this group, list the guys you have dated, are currently interested in, or have some reason to believe are your most likely candidates for marriage.

2. Friends, but no romance. List the men you know as friends, but don't consider to be romantic options. Include not only current friends at work, but think back to other periods of your life, such as college. Who were your male friends?

3. Casual acquaintances. List the men you hardly know, but might want to know better: guys you pass at work, brothers of friends, a man you see at church from time to time.

4. Guys I'd like to meet. List here anyone who interests you from afar—perhaps a man you've read about or a man someone has told you about. These are the men who probably inhabit your dreams.

Keep adding to these lists. You'll be surprised at who begins to pop into your mind. Perhaps you'll remember a high school friend's big brother. Or a co-worker will mention an old boyfriend who seems more your type than hers.

Look at your list at least once a week and analyze, to the best of your abilities, which of these men have the characteristics you are most interested in. Try to remain as open-minded as possible. Naturally, you have less information about the third and fourth categories of guys.

Possibly because they don't see the whole picture, many single women concentrate much of their energies on these last two categories and fail to look at guys they know well. Yet the truth is that the greatest opportunity for finding someone to share your life with is probably in the first two groups of men: *Guys you already know!*

Under the strategy section in your notebook write the following action steps:

1. *Go out with more guys who are not immediately attractive to me.*

2. *Analyze the guys I know more objectively.*

3. *Get to know the guys I know casually, so I know if they are prospects.*

4. *Meet the guys I think I may be interested in.*

Remember that you should concentrate 90 percent of your efforts on the first two categories and 10 percent on the last. When Janet reached this stage in her strategic planning, she stopped and said, "I'm willing to take another look at the guys I know, but what if they aren't interested in me?"

"Maybe you just need to help them see you in a new way," I suggested. "If we were doing a marketing plan, we'd call this 'product analysis.' But that sounds so unexciting. Let's start a new section in your notebook called 'The Real Me.'"

"Now that sounds like fun," Janet agreed. We were laughing as we left breakfast together, and it occurred to me that Janet was looking more like the person she really was. She had a twinkle in her eye, a bounce in her step, and as she walked past one of the waiters, he gave her a second look, clearly finding her attractive. I smiled to myself as I thought of just how far Janet had come in just a few weeks.

CHAPTER FIVE

Getting to Know You

om Selleck had been named "America's Most Eligible Bachelor," "the most handsome man in the world," and "every woman's dream date." Not only is he nice looking, but he also has an incredible physique, a great sense of humor, a warm personality, several million dollars, and a red Ferrari.

Jillie Mack has been most often described as a "British dancer and actress." She is neither famous nor wealthy. She is not a classically beautiful woman and is often described as "cute." Yet when Tom Selleck met Jillie Mack, by all accounts he was smitten. After three years of dating, they were married and seem to be living happily ever after.

Tom Selleck looks at his wife as if she were the most beautiful woman in the world. Jillie Mack holds her head high, looks confident and happy, and seems totally unaware that she isn't gorgeous. Perhaps you already know the moral of this story. . . .

When I asked Janet to list what she considered her good and bad qualities, she wrote two lists, one long, the other short. Like many women, she was able to go into great detail about her negatives: mousy hair, eyes too close together, too fat, silly laugh, etc. On the positive side, she listed one physical characteristic—nice hands—and character qualities like loyalty, honesty, and sense of humor.

When I pressed Janet for more positives, she added "small feet." "This is terrible!" I said, to which Janet replied, "I guess I don't have much to work with, do I?"

"You have plenty to work with," I said. "But without an attitude adjustment your only hope is to find a guy who is looking for a loyal woman with small feet and nice hands!"

Janet laughed. "I can see your point," she said. "But I am who I am. I can't change that, and I can't pretend to be someone I'm not."

YOU'RE AS BEAUTIFUL AS YOU FEEL

I didn't totally agree with Janet about who she was and her possibilities for changing. On a sheet of paper, I wrote *NEGATIVES*. Under it I labeled two columns—*"Improve"* and *"Ignore."* On another piece of paper, I wrote *POSITIVES*. Then I divided a third sheet of paper into three sections which I entitled: *I. Attention, II. Acttraction,* and *III. Attachment* (see p. 175).

We were ready to go to work on Janet.

We began on the negative sheet, since that came so easily to her. One by one we went through what she considered to be her negatives and placed them in the appropriate column. The fact that she was short we placed under "ignore." Her close set eyes we placed halfway between "ignore" and "improve" with the understanding that a few makeup lessons could change her perspective on her eyes.

NEGATIVES		
<u>Improve</u>		<u>Ignore</u>
Mousy hair		Too short
Too fat	Close set eyes	
Silly laugh		

The rest of Janet's negatives—mousy hair, too fat, silly laugh, etc.—were lining up almost entirely under "improve." Janet looked depressed. "I guess I've got to get to work," she said.

"Not yet," I insisted. "We need to work on the positives first."

After some coaxing, Janet added eye color (blue), hair color (blond), and nice legs to her list of positives. I insisted she place *petite* on the list. Her shortness was a positive to most guys. The only reason she disliked it was that she had a hard time controlling her weight and wished she were taller so she could balance out her figure.

Next Janet wanted to know about the "Three A's"— attention, attraction, and attachment. I explained that during the past week I had been thinking about the way most relationships develop. It seemed to me that certain characteristics were more important at different stages of the relationship. For example, Janet's physical qualities were important in the first stage, when she was just getting to know a guy. Both her positive and negative physical attributes would play an important part in getting a guy's attention in the first place.

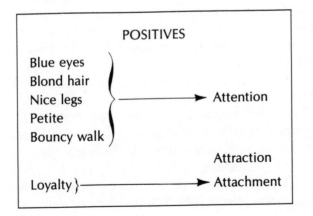

Stage two began when a guy had definitely noticed her and was beginning to be interested on more than a superficial level. Stage three was when a couple became serious. At this stage, they had basically accepted each other, and problems would occur only if they had a conflict of values or if certain qualities seemed too negative to accept.

I suggested to Janet that we try to highlight three positive qualities for each stage of relationships. For example, loyalty, which she considered to be one of her best qualities, was something that could not be truly appreciated until late in stage two and during stage three. It was a quality that could cement a relationship, but would rarely make a guy ask her out in the first place.

Furthermore, if on her first date with a guy she tried to show how loyal she was, she'd probably come across as too serious or even possessive. She would have to know a guy for a while before loyalty could even be recognized as a positive quality.

"I just hate dealing with the superficial aspects of relationships," Janet complained. "Why can't a guy learn to appreciate me for who I really am?"

"He can, and eventually will," I promised Janet. But I reminded her that she, too, had just admitted that when looking for guys, she often went no further in developing a relationship if he weren't physically attractive. Yet when she really analyzed it, Janet knew that the physical side wasn't important.

"But how do I know how other people see me?" Janet asked.

"Why don't you just ask them?" I suggested.

Janet decided to consult some trusted friends, relatives, and even old boyfriends and ask them what they considered to be her strengths and weaknesses. I urged her to view this as a research project, not a personal encounter session and to phrase it as such to the people she talked to.

A week later, Janet came back in great spirits. An old boyfriend had told her that she had beautiful eyes and that was what attracted him to her. When she asked him why the relationship hadn't continued, he admitted that he felt put off by her bluntness at times. During the week of thinking about it, Janet realized that her positive quality of honesty might be a negative as well. But she also knew that her eyes really were a positive trait and felt free to admit that she liked them, even if they were a bit too close together.

A friend told Janet she always liked her "bouncy walk." Another pointed out her spontaneity. Janet began to develop a more accurate image of herself based on others' perceptions. And when several people suggested that she might want to lose a few pounds, the weight issue became more focused.

Janet had been assuming that the extra weight she'd been carrying around was well disguised. But now she realized it was getting in the way of what others saw as well as the way she saw herself.

Blond hair wasn't mentioned by anyone, even though I'd always admired the beautiful color. When I suggested that wearing it short as she did might be hiding a good quality, she said, "I've always worn it short because I thought short girls should have short hair."

She decided to try growing it longer.

We were ready to add some specifics to our strategy sheet. "Lose ten pounds" and "grow out hair" were the obvious ones. Then we went back to our sheet of positives and looked at the stages.

Under stage one we put hair, eyes, legs, and bouncy walk. Under stage two we put sense of humor, laugh, spontaneity, taste in clothes. Under stage three we listed faith, honesty, loyalty, and patience.

As Janet embarked upon her diet, she did it with new determination, knowing that she needed to lose weight for a specific reason—not to be someone she wasn't, but, in fact, to be seen as the wonderful person she was.

If you are serious about finding your Mr. Right, don't skip this stage of self-analysis. We all have blind spots about ourselves. Some are left over from childhood messages we heard. Others come from fear that the truth is too painful. But knowing how others see you can be a great relief.

Most women are too hard on themselves. Like Janet, you may be able to quickly list the negatives about yourself but have a hard time adding positives to the list. Yet, as you will discover in later chapters, men need to know that you like yourself. The better you feel about yourself, the better men will feel about you.

You may know a woman who seems to attract men, yet is neither stunning nor brilliant. But chances are she has that "extra something" that men seem to notice. That something is confidence. Even if you don't have it naturally, you need to learn to fake it if you want to be successful with men.

One of the most confident women I know confessed to me that she felt ugly and unloved as a teenager. She struggled with self-doubt and even contemplated suicide at one point. Pictures of her from the past show a sad looking, not very attractive young woman. Yet it is clear that this is the same woman that today men and women alike describe as beautiful.

When I asked this woman what made the difference in her life, she told me that her mother talked to her very seriously one day about her future. And then she told her that whenever she felt scared and unlovely, she should stand up tall and walk into a situation "like she owned the joint." She began to try it and discovered that the old saying was true: You are as beautiful as you feel.

How Can You Learn to Feel Confident?

1. Develop an accurate picture of yourself based on how others see you.

2. Improve what you can.

3. Ignore what you can't improve or minimize its importance.

4. Accentuate your positive characteristics at the appropriate stage of a relationship.

5. If you don't feel confident, act as if you do.

Developing Your Personal Résumé

What are my best qualities? _____

_____

What would I like to change? _____

_____

What do others like about me? _____

_____

What qualities get men's ATTENTION?

Figure   Smile   _____

Hair   Walk   _____

Face   _____   _____

What qualities ATTRACT men?

Voice   _____

Sense of humor   _____

Laugh   _____

Ability to make him   _____
   feel important

What qualities form ATTACHMENTS?

Sensitivity   Faith   _____

Loyalty   Interests   _____

Being upbeat   _____   _____

♥

CHAPTER SIX

A Self-Improvement Plan

$\mathbf{M}$y breakfasts with Janet made me more and more curious about men's views on a number of issues. So I decided to begin a research project of my own to learn what guys were thinking. One day I sat down with a group of nice looking, personable, single men who seemed to be most single women's ideal type of guy.

"Describe your ideal woman," I asked. I waited for a few moments, then coaxed, "Tell me how she would look." Their answers surprised me.

"She wouldn't be really beautiful," one said. Even though all of the guys were nice looking themselves, each shook his head in agreement. "She would just look nice and friendly and fun," he continued. "I wouldn't want someone who looked like she just wanted to sit in a chair and not get dirty."

"She wouldn't wear too much makeup," another said.

"I'd like someone who looked sort of athletic. Not a real jock—just someone I could go out and run with."

When it got right down to it, the guys weren't looking for Miss America. They weren't even looking for a woman who was beautiful or had a great figure. They were looking for a woman who was attractive to them because she had a certain way about her, what one guy described as "that special something" that makes a woman stand out.

Yet when I asked women who were unhappy with their dating life to tell me why they didn't date, many said they didn't think they were pretty enough. Not one of these women was distinctly unattractive. In fact, some had natural beauty that they seemed to ignore.

When I asked a group of men to show me the women in their church group who were particularly popular, I was amazed to discover that they were not stunning or glamorous. Some were basically plain; yet each one had a way about her, a sense of herself, that seemed to invite interest. Where do you find that special something?

First, the good news. You don't have to be a natural beauty to have it. In fact, really beautiful women often scare the average guy away. You don't have to have a great deal of money. Some of the women who spend the most on their makeup and wardrobe are the least attractive to men.

What it does take is an understanding of what is attractive to men and an approach to your appearance that says you care about what men think. If that sounds simple, remember that most women dress for other women. They wear clothes that are fashionable, hair styles that are current, makeup that is "the latest."

Men rarely care about those standards. In fact, current fashion is often aimed at creating a look that is more theatrical than feminine. That's not to say that you shouldn't dress fashionably. But when selecting what you wear, don't try so much to dress for success or for the other women you know. Consider whether the men you know would like it. Remember what type of clothing gets you compliments from men. Take a look at yourself in a full-length mirror before going out the door each morning. Do you look like a woman who would get a second glance from men walking down the street?

It might sound basic, but take a close look at your appearance. We all lead such busy lives that it is easy for us to forget to really look at ourselves, yet this is a key step to our physical attractiveness. A friend of mine I'll call Lynn had many positive qualities but didn't seem to notice her dandruff problem until she heard a man jokingly call her Snow White. Another friend had a wonderful wardrobe, but discovered that men found her clothes "severe." We could all use a quick appearance checkup. Why not review the following areas?

1. Grooming. This is a basic and very general category that many women take for granted. Yet you need to do a regular checkup here to make sure you're not losing points with men without realizing it.

Whenever you go out the door is your hair clean and fresh smelling? Or have you decided that it's only Saturday, so no one will notice that you skipped a shampoo? Even if you've never had dandruff, be sure to check your shoulders periodically. And change shampoos from time to time to keep the bounce in your hair.

What about your deodorant? If you've used the same brand for a long time, it might be important to be sure it's still working—especially during the summer months. And don't forget to brush your teeth and gargle. An upset stomach or even a cup of coffee can leave your mouth smelling sour. You don't want to get close to a man for the first time only to leave him with a negative impression.

Dirty hands and nails are another "turnoff" for men. If you've read the newspaper on the way to work, be sure to wash the newsprint off of your hands. And if you wear nail polish, don't ever go out in public with even one nail chipped or peeling. You're better off never wearing polish at all than having your whole look ruined by a chipped nail.

If you're a coffee or tea drinker, be sure to have your teeth cleaned regularly so you don't have a dingy smile. A smile is one of your most valuable assets. Be sure it's bright and sparkling.

2. Weight. One of the biggest concerns of single women is their weight. As one woman told me, "I eat because I'm not dating. Then I'm not dating because I'm overweight." If you do think you have a weight problem, first recognize that most men don't notice ten extra pounds if you dress properly. Don't mope around worrying about your figure. Go on a sensible diet, but live your life as if you've already lost weight.

If you're more than ten pounds overweight DO SOMETHING ABOUT IT TODAY. As a graduate of several diet plans, I highly recommend that you enroll in Weight Watchers. It's not just for grossly overweight older women. Almost every class has young and old, those who need to lose ten pounds and those who need to lose 100. It is a sensible, realistic plan that will help you take the weight off and keep it off. It will teach you good eating habits that will last a lifetime.

If you do go on a diet, don't talk about it—especially around men. It will only make them more aware of your figure flaws. If you really think about it, you'll realize that some of the women who are popular with men are overweight. They just don't act like it's a problem. While you're dieting, imagine the slim you of your goal weight. You'll be surprised by the way others begin to treat you.

An exercise program can do wonders for a weight problem and can also help you meet men. (See the suggestions in chapter eight.) It will also improve your outlook on life and give you a tangible aura of energy, which men find very interesting.

If you're more than ten pounds underweight, you may need professional help in order to gain weight. Although most guys won't notice if you are slightly too thin, a woman who is too bony or angular simply won't be attractive to most men.

3. Hair. Although short hair is popular with many women, guys have a definite preference for longer hair. Some psychologists suggest that it is still a very primal way for men to distinguish between the sexes; others say that men fantasize about running their fingers through a woman's hair.

Some women look great with short hair. But unless you have a really pretty face and a good figure, you're "safer" with long hair. Long shiny hair can help minimize a less than perfect face and balance out your figure. It can be worn in serious and not so serious ways; it can be played with flirtatiously; and it can be curled or worn straight. Although long hair takes more time to care for, it is a great asset with men. If you don't usually wear your hair long, try growing it shoulder length or longer and see what reaction you get from men.

Whatever length you wear your hair, steer away from hairspray, gels, or mousses; guys specifically dislike teased hair or hair that looks stiff and unatural.

Hair color preferences vary, but blonds still have more fun when it comes to most men. If you have brown hair, consider giving it blond highlights. If you have darker hair, a henna rinse can make your hair shinier and give it a red or dark brown tone. Black hair is really popular with some men and redheads seem to be enjoying renewed popularity. Make the most of your hair color, whatever the shade. Have a professional evaluate your hair and suggest ways to make the color more lively.

Do find a hair professional who can see you regularly and work with you overtime. It may save you a few dollars to go to a "quick cut" salon and see the next available operator, but why risk the look of your hair when it is such an important asset?

4. Makeup. "I hate it when women wear makeup," one man told me as I interviewed him about his likes and dislikes. I asked him if the makeup I was wearing was offensive, and he said that he didn't believe I was wearing any. When I told him that I was wearing mascara, blusher, lipstick and eye shadow, he was shocked. "It's the goopy kind I hate," he explained. From that and other conversations I've had with men, I have drawn the conclusion that it's too much makeup that causes men to shudder, but properly applied makeup isn't noticeable to most men.

Men seem to have an overwhelming fear of having makeup smeared on them. If you wear foundation, be sure it's not too heavy or cakey looking. Don't wear so much powder that you look unnatural. And don't wear bright lipstick that looks as if it would leave a red mark on anything you come near. Eye makeup can easily look overdone if you wear blues or greens or frosted shades, so confine your daytime makeup to earth tones when possible.

If you are fair skinned, you probably need to wear some makeup in order to keep from blending in with the background. If you have dark skin or hair, you may need less makeup, especially during the day. You may want to consult a professional at a makeup counter in a department store to help you find the right shade. But remember that people who sell makeup will want you to wear more than you may actually want for a natural look.

5. Fragrance. Find a fragrance that is soft and not too strong, then wear it regularly. Don't switch off. Let it become known as "your" perfume. Men love to associate a certain scent with you and will subconsciously enjoy remembering you by the lingering scent after you leave.

6. Jewelry. Single women have to be careful about the kind of jewelry they wear because men are not very discerning about the significance of different types of jewelry. If I were single, I wouldn't wear any rings. Many men can't remember if an engagement ring is worn on the right or left hand. They see any ring with a stone as a sign that the woman is seeing another man.

Men also tend to view heart necklaces and jeweled bracelets or necklaces as signs that a woman has a serious boyfriend who has given her the item as a gift. Why risk losing the attention of a man who misunderstands your jewelry? It may sound silly, but I know several men who have viewed a woman's jewelry as a sign that she is "taken."

7. Posture. At one time or another we have all been reminded to "stand up straight." But if you haven't checked your posture lately, stand in front of a full-length mirror, pull your shoulders back, and see what standing tall can do for your looks. An easy way to remember to have good posture is to think of a string attached to the top of your head pulling you up. Your chin will lift slightly, your shoulders will pull back, your stomach will tuck in. You'll look and feel confident. Even if you're tall, don't think slouching will make you look shorter. It only will make you look sloppy.

Now think about the way you walk. Is it stiff, shuffling, forceful? Think about what your walk says about you. Then practice different walks for your different moods. Try walking in a way that says you're happy or feeling playful. Think about how you walk in high heels versus the way you walk in tennis shoes. How do you think you appear to others as you walk past them? Do you slouch and shuffle? Do you "bounce"? Do your arms swing wildly? Work on your walk and learn to develop a nonverbal way of communicating who you are.

8. Voice. Have you ever heard yourself on a recording and been startled to learn how others hear you? Your voice is an important factor in how others judge you initially. Try recording yourself during a phone call, then play back the tape and listen critically to your voice. Do you use sloppy language ("um," "you know," "like")? Is your voice energetic or monotoned? Is your tone high-pitched or shrill?

There are several books available to help you work on your voice. For most women their voices could be improved by dropping the pitch and speaking more slowly and distinctly. Try working on your voice and see if others begin to react differently to you. Often the stereotypes that we have about people have less to do with what they say than how they say it.

9. *Clothing*. We've already discussed the fact that women often dress more for each other than for men. So your aim will need to be to learn how to dress for men. Let me hasten to say, however, that dressing for men does not mean wearing clinging or revealing outfits. It simply means wearing softer clothes rather than clothes that are severely tailored. Think about what you wear that results in compliments from men. Is there something that these clothes have in common?

If you usually dress formally, try wearing looser, more casual clothes and see how men react. Try wearing unexpected colors. Red seems to be a favorite with some men, while others seem to specifically like blue. Black may seem sophisticated to some men, but others might find it funereal. Don't be afraid to experiment. If you have a male friend, see if he'd be willing to go along on a shopping trip and tell you how he reacts to different clothes you try on. You may be surprised at the male perspective on fashion.

10. *Attitude*. Finally, remember that attitude is more important than anything you do to change or enhance your physical appearance. Try walking into a room with a smile on your face, your head held tall, and the thought *I feel really beautiful*. The reaction you will get may startle you if you typically try to melt into the scenery. You truly are as beautiful as you feel. Others will sense your outlook and be attracted to you. But first you have to believe in yourself.

cathy®

by Cathy Guisewite

♥

CHAPTER SEVEN

The Approachability Factor

Ohne day Janet introduced me to a friend of hers named Ann. Ann was a pretty, confident woman in her late twenties. When I met her, she was wearing a beautiful suit that complemented her figure. After we talked for a while, Janet explained the real reason she was introducing me to Ann. "Ann doesn't date, either," Janet explained. "None of her friends understand why. So I thought maybe you would have some ideas."

Ann was involved in public relations and had learned to be upbeat and positive on the job. She was fairly clear about what she wanted in a man and was quite open-minded to men from different backgrounds as long as they shared her faith. It seemed that Ann had done everything right, yet she still hadn't met the man of her dreams.

It was clear that she was physically attractive and had made the most of her natural assets. She worked hard at staying in shape and looking good in her clothes.

Before I had spent time interviewing men, I would have been perplexed by Ann's problem. She was attractive and confident. She seemed to have it all together by the standards of magazines and ads for the modern woman. But what I observed in the short time I knew her was that, when it came to men, she was going about things all wrong.

"Ann, maybe you just need to meet more guys," I suggested. "But I also think we may need to improve your approachability factor."

"What in the world is that?" she asked.

I explained to her that she was, by most standards, the image of the successful modern day woman. She looked like she had it all together. She seemed to know where she was going. She also probably scared many guys off.

"It's true that some guys have said I seem 'intimidating,'" she said. "But I never knew what they meant."

"I think it's a compliment, in a way," Janet offered. "But I also think that most guys don't have enough confidence to deal with someone who seems as 'together' as you do."

"But I don't want men to see me that way," Ann said. "What can I do?"

Janet, Ann, and I met for lunch one day the next week and all brought our ideas of what Ann could do to solve her problem. Some of our ideas were basic, but after we wrote down our list we discovered that there were at least ten "cures" for a low approachability factor.

TEN WAYS TO BECOME MORE APPROACHABLE

1. Flirt. Give up the idea that you are being true to who you are by not flirting or letting a guy know you are interested. You're willing to improve your job skills, your tennis game, and your mind. Why not learn to improve your ability to relate to others? Flirting got a bad name somewhere along the line. It began to be associated with the most outrageous caricatures of Marilyn Monroe-type women who threw themselves at men.

But flirting is a natural way of beginning the "courting" process. It is a way of showing a man that you may be interested in him. It helps ease the awkward times in the early stages of a relationship. It doesn't have to be manipulative. In many ways, it's a painless way to honestly say, "I'm interested in you."

Many women say that they just can't flirt. Anyone can flirt. They just may not feel comfortable doing so with the opposite sex. I've seen women who claim that they have no flirting abilities have a great time with children—encouraging them, teasing them, and playing games. Most of the patterns that you use when playing with children are very similar to adult flirtations. Your voice becomes softer and more playful, you are more appreciative of positive qualities, and you listen carefully to what the other person is saying, either following with a question or making an encouraging remark. Some people can flirt just with their eyes or through a smile.

If you are uncomfortable with the idea of flirtation, here are some tips that might help:

- *Flirtation can be subtle.* You don't have to bat your eyelashes, feel a man's muscles, or tell him he's Superman. But if you are too subtle most men won't even notice. Try out different styles of flirting until you feel comfortable. Observe women who are successful flirts. What do they do? How do guys respond?

- *Role play.* Pretend you are someone else and act out the flirtations you have observed.

- *Practice on friends and relatives.* Women who are good at flirtations with men often have a flirtatious style with everyone. They flirt, in a sense, with girlfriends, co-workers, even the postman. Try being more friendly and playful with everyone in your life.

- *Forget about yourself.* Remember that flirting has more to do with appreciating the other person than drawing attention to yourself. Jean Giradoux, a wise French man, once observed, "When you see a woman who can go nowhere without a staff of admirers, it is not so much because they think she is beautiful, it is because she has told them they are handsome."

- *Work at it.* Flirting comes naturally to some people, but it is a learned art for most of us. Remind yourself each morning to work at flirting. Record in your notebook the flirtation skills that you are learning and what results they bring from different types of men.

2. Don't Be Proud. Pride is not a virtue, especially in relating to men. One day Janet and I were discussing a man and I encouraged her to let him know she was interested in him. "But I don't want him to think I'm chasing him," she said.

"So what if he thinks you're chasing him?" I challenged her. "What's the worst thing that can happen? Probably the worst is that he is not interested and lets you know it. If that happens you're ahead of the game. You at least know that you should move on to someone else and stop wasting your time."

"I never thought of it that way," Janet admitted.

When I interviewed guys about their feelings regarding women who "chased" them, most said they couldn't even remember it happening, but wished it would. Furthermore, they didn't say they'd be put off by it, even if the girl were not of interest to them at all. They would be flattered. Some even said they might think again about the woman or take her out once, just to see what she was really like.

I remember watching a rather nice looking guy in my singles group at church being openly pursued by a very ordinary woman. We all thought she didn't have a chance in the world. Today they are married and have three children. Now that I know them well, I realize that he is very shy and probably would have remained unmarried to this day if she hadn't pursued him. She would have saved her pride, but lost out on her Mr. Right.

I heard about another woman who had been casually dating a man for months, but the relationship wasn't going anywhere, even though she was interested in him. She was

cathy®

by Cathy Guisewite

too proud to show her true feelings and was afraid he'd reject her. Finally, she knocked on his door one evening and blurted out that she loved him and wanted them to seriously work at the relationship. They were married six months later.

3. Smile. If you do nothing else, learn to walk into every setting with a smile on your face. Practice smiles in front of the mirror. Learn to wear a slight smile, even as you drive your car. Train your mouth to turn up and your eyes to sparkle.

Observe other people and notice what their faces look like as they sit on the bus, work at their desks, or listen to a sermon. Most frown. And when they frown, they look unapproachable because they appear to be deep in thought, angry, or concerned. A person with a smile looks open, warm, honest. She seems to invite conversation and to automatically accept you when you look at her.

When you smile, the natural response is for the other person to smile back. In doing so, even before a word is spoken, there is an automatic connection. You've probably heard the expression, "Laugh and the world laughs with you; weep and you weep alone." You can easily substitute *smile* and *frown* in that quote and come up with a saying that you should place on your mirror, on your desk at work, and on the dashboard of your car: "Smile and the world smiles with you; frown and you frown alone."

Smile as you listen to a speaker, read your mail, watch TV. Make a smile the natural posture of your face. If you feel awkward at first, warm up to it by wearing a slight smile the entire time you are doing your grocery shopping. Then practice walking into your office with a big smile every morning. Set a little alarm at your desk to remind you to smile before you go out for lunch.

Try smiling as much as you can for one week and see what happens. You may be shocked by how many people approach you and how many people comment on how happy you seem.

4. Go Casual. When in doubt, adopt a more casual style. Many women who work in offices scrimp and save in order to afford some nice-looking business clothes to make them look professional at the office. That's fine, but when it comes to off hours or situations where you hope to meet men, wear a dress instead of a suit, bright colors instead of navy and gray, and select something that's more draped or flowing than tailored.

That doesn't mean you should wear clothing that is suggestive or sexy. But men admit to being turned off when a woman wears a suit on a date. They want her to look "soft" (their description) and like she can be fun and spontaneous —an image hardly enhanced by the tailored look.

Although men are stereotyped as liking clinging clothes, many men say that they think a baggy sweatshirt or loose t-shirt is "sexy." Wear comfortable clothes that are neat, clean, and coordinated, but don't make the mistake of wearing stiff-looking casual clothes. In general, don't wear tight clothes, especially if you are overweight. A man may wonder about your figure under a loose dress, but he'll know the details if the dress is too tight.

When it comes to hair, men like it "soft, long, flowing" (the three most-often-used adjectives by men) and dislike hair that is styled. They especially dislike hair that is sprayed into a style, and most guys do not like the look of hair that is gelled into place.

Ironically, many of the current hair and clothing styles are meant to please other women and not men. If you have a good male friend, ask him to rate the clothes you wear as attractive or unattractive.

I've learned that the clothes I bring home that are "the latest style" often do very little for my husband. His famous line is "Is it supposed to look like that?" Yet some of the clothes that I consider less stylish are his favorites: a loose blue sweater, a dress with a long, flowing skirt, and a skirt and sweater in a pretty turquoise.

Am I wrong to dress to please my husband? Absolutely not. If he likes what I'm wearing, he feels more positively toward me and is pleased that I want to make him happy. Is it wrong to wear clothes that are more attractive to men than other women? Only if you don't care much about going out but would rather be voted the most stylish woman in the office.

5. Be Modest. Downplay your job and your accomplishments everywhere but on your résumé. Many single women have exciting careers and have poured their energy into their jobs. But too often they make the mistake of going on a date and acting like it's a job interview. Don't talk about your job, especially to men, unless you are asked about it. Just use simple good manners by always making an effort to talk less about yourself and more about the other person.

And remember that men often feel confused by the changing role of women. Many admit that they assume most women want a career instead of marriage. When they meet a woman who is "caught up" in her career, they assume that she is more interested in it than in them.

That doesn't mean you have to misrepresent what you do or your interest in it. Loving your job is fine. Talking about how great you are is not. Just imagine that you are introduced to Sandra Day O'Connor and are seated next to her at a dinner party. Obviously she has an important job and is interested in it. But if she spends the evening talking about the latest cases before the Supreme Court and how well she phrased her opinions, you will leave the party thinking she's a bore and has very few interests beyond the Supreme Court, and you will probably feel inferior.

However, if she asks you about your job and spends the evening getting to know you, you will probably mention to all of your friends that she is not only a very important person, but also smart, fun, and multi-dimensional. She won't have compromised her position. In fact, she will have enhanced her reputation. She also will have shown that she is not so involved in her career that she doesn't have the ability to relate to other people who are not judges.

6. Expand Your Horizons. Learn to be a more interesting person. Begin by understanding a principle taught by Dale Carnegie as one of the cornerstones of human relationships: "Become genuinely interested in other people." By doing so, you'll find more and more people become interested in you.

If it sounds like strange logic, remember that the world is full of people who know more than you do about a number of topics. Emerson said, "Every man I meet is in some way my superior; and in that I can learn of him." Look around you at the office, at church, even at the supermarket. What can you learn from the people around you?

Learn to ask questions, then listen—really listen—to the answers. Draw people out. Ask them about their background, their attitudes, their dreams. Offer them hypothetical situations and ask how they would respond.

Push yourself to learn new skills, explore new fields, or develop new interests. Take up a new sport. Even if you're not terribly coordinated, you can take up bicycling and go on short weekend trips. Or you can learn to sail if you live near an ocean or lake.

Expanding your horizons doesn't come naturally. It's much easier to sit at home and watch television than to go to a lecture on architecture. It's safer never to talk to the person sitting next to you at church than to introduce yourself and ask where he's from. But every time you take the easy route, your world shrinks a bit. On the other hand, every time you walk into a new situation or get to know someone new, you grow as a person and your universe expands.

Expanding your horizons is a bit like smiling—it's a learned skill that anyone can do. You don't have to be talented or beautiful to be interested in the world around you. But the more interested you become in other things, the more interesting you will become to other people.

7. Have Fun. Add whimsy to your life. Look for ways to show people that you have a sense of humor and that you don't take yourself too seriously. Wear bright yellow boots on a rainy day or buy an umbrella in an unexpected color. Pull your hair into a high, swinging pony tail or occasionally use bright barrettes to hold your hair back.

Wear high top tennis shoes or knee socks with loafers. Buy some funny earrings or wear a pin that is more cute than serious. Buy a coffee cup for your desk at work that says something about you—but be careful what it says! Avoid cups that indicate neuroses or talk about being single. Instead, use a cup with a funny slogan or shaped like a pink flamingo, or anything that shows your sense of humor.

Let people see that you can have fun and forget about yourself. Give them the message that you can laugh at the many ironies of life and that you will be able to laugh with them, not at them, if something embarrassing happens. Guys, especially, like to know that a woman will not laugh at them if they do something silly.

8. Be Vulnerable. For years women have been hearing the message that if they are going to be taken seriously in a business atmosphere, they must act tough. They aren't to show emotions or softness in any way. This may be good advice for the board room, but it doesn't get a woman dates.

That doesn't mean that you should openly weep in public or put your emotions on display. However, it's important to switch off your invulnerable side when you leave the office. Or even better, learn to be vulnerable—even at the office—in controlled ways.

Concentrate on being warm, caring, and concerned, no matter where you are. Don't try to underrate your own problems, but don't dwell on them either. Instead of pretending that your mounting work load is totally under control, admit to a friend that you're having "one of those days." Don't complain about it endlessly. Just let people know that you have tough times, too.

Empathize with co-workers who are having a hard time. Let them know that you understand their concerns and share them at times yourself. Learn to be a good listener, but don't become an office gossip.

Bring enough of your personal life into the office so people know that you're human, but don't discuss problems in detail. It's fine to admit that you were embarrassed on the bus when you tripped and landed in someone's lap. It's not all right, however, to talk about the messy fights you have with your sister.

In order to develop relationships with people around you, you need to share part of yourself with others. Share stories that are funny or that show your vulnerabilities without making you seem foolish or weak. But also be willing to let others know that you are clumsy or absent-minded at times. If you seem too distant, or too good to be true, you will cut off the possibility of relationships with others.

9. Be Mysterious. This may sound like the opposite of vulnerability, but it isn't really. You want people to think you are open and warm, but you don't want them to think they know everything about you. Men love to think that women are mysterious. It makes them want to get to know you better and find out what motivates you.

When I asked men to describe their worst dates, they often said that the woman was "boring" and that she didn't have much to offer. Yet some of the women they were describing had so much going for them that it was clearly a problem of perception rather than reality.

To successfully create an air of mystery, a woman has to start out with confidence. It may help to play a role. Think of yourself as Catherine Deneuve, a woman who is the epitome of beauty and mystery. How would she act on a date? She certainly wouldn't chatter on about her interests, tell her life story in the first ten minutes, or complain about the weather. Neither should you.

Don't be too predictable. If you always go to lunch with the same gang, try eating alone for a change. Take a different route to work, or ride the bus instead of driving. Do something just to be different, and then don't tell anyone about it. Begin to have your own little secrets, not to be deceitful, but to learn to be self-contained. Begin to think of yourself as an interesting person, but don't feel a need to make anyone else believe it. Without even knowing it, you will begin to develop an air of mystery.

10. Forget about Yourself. Being self-contained does not mean being self-absorbed. One of the greatest traps of the single life is becoming too self-absorbed. Many single women spend their time thinking too much about themselves, their lack of dates, and their present and future life. Being self-absorbed feeds itself to the point where you might as well be carrying a sign that says, "I'm just interested in me."

Even though they talk about men and about wanting to date, many women have simply become unapproachable because their minds and actions are all directed inward. Breaking this pattern of self-absorption can be difficult, especially because it becomes comfortable after a while. But here are a few tips to help you retrain your mind to focus outward, especially when you are alone.

- As you drive to work in the morning, begin to think about others.

- Read books, especially biographies, that teach you about other people.

- Volunteer to work with the disabled persons, with children, or with the elderly.

- Pray less about getting a husband, or losing weight, or any of the other self-directed concerns, and more about others.

- Thank God for all He has given you and ask Him to give you a grateful heart. Then ask Him to help you help others.

If you need some inspiration to get you started, read *I Love the Word Impossible* by Ann Kiemel (Tyndale, 1978). Ann is a woman who accomplished amazing things during her single years. By serving in her church and with children in her neighborhood, she met people from all across the country—including the man who became her husband.

Perhaps some of the advice in this chapter sounds "unliberated" in this day and age. I'm all in favor of women being all they can be and being rewarded for it. Yet so many women have embraced the concepts that lead to professional success to the exclusion of personal happiness. As Janet observed, "What good is success if you have no one to share it with?"

Can you be both personally and professionally successful? Absolutely. But you have to remember that developing your personal skills takes the same kind of time and energy that you'd use in developing your job skills.

When Janet's friend, Ann, began to actually use some of these suggestions, she was surprised by the reactions. One man said, "I was always afraid to talk to you before." A woman in her office confessed that she never realized Ann had a sense of humor. Ann didn't really change very much about herself. But the change in her social life was nothing short of dramatic.

"Sometimes I'm sorry we ever encouraged Ann," Janet said jokingly. "She seems to date more guys now than anyone I know."

"Don't worry, Janet," I assured her. "Wait until we start brainstorming about ways for you to meet guys."

♥

CHAPTER EIGHT

Why Can't a Man Think More Like a Woman?

J ulia had a crush on Carl. It was clear to everyone who worked with her—except him. Whenever he walked past her desk, she looked up hopefully. When he handed her something to type, she stammered and blushed. If he entered the room, she forgot what she was saying and glanced furtively in his direction.

We all liked Julia and were rooting for her in her quest for Carl's attention. A quiet, capable woman in her early thirties, she wasn't a "knockout," but she had pretty eyes, dressed neatly, and was a loyal and tireless co-worker. We were sure that one day Carl would see what a wonderful person she really was.

Carl was a widower, ten years her senior. He was nice looking, although his hair was thinning and his middle thickening. He didn't seem to be dating anyone regularly, yet he walked past Julia every day without seeming to notice her.

Finally I couldn't stand it any longer. One day while I was having a cup of coffee with Carl, the subject of the office Christmas party came up. When I asked him who he was bringing, he said he thought he'd come alone. "Why don't you bring Julia?" I asked casually.

He looked at me blankly for a minute and then said, "You mean Julia in accounting? I thought she was married."

"What made you think she was married?" I asked, totally flabbergasted by the confusion.

"She *looks* married," he responded. And then after a minute he said, "She has pictures of her kids on her desk." I laughed as I pointed out that the pictures were of her nieces, to whom she was a devoted and loving aunt.

Carl wasn't convinced. "She wears a ring," he said, somewhat defensively. I thought for a moment and then realized he was talking about the birthstone ring that she wore on her right hand.

"Carl, that's not a wedding ring. Besides, she wears it on her right hand," I said.

"I never was very good about remembering those kinds of things," he said, and I shook my head, thinking of the complicated computer programs he developed and implemented. "She *is* a nice person," he said, and I began to grow hopeful. "But I think she's too old for me."

"Too old for you!" I practically yelled. "She's at least ten years younger than you. What makes you think she's too old?"

"She has gray hair," Carl said, almost pouting now.

I realized that Carl still saw himself as the college football star. He was insulted to think that he would be expected to date someone whose hair was turning gray, even though his was almost gone. I realized the fundamental problem keeping Julia and Carl from discovering each other was the age-old difference between men's perception and women's perception.

It reminded me of the scene from "My Fair Lady" in which Professor Higgins exclaims, "Why can't a woman be more like a man?" In this case, I wanted to yell, "Why can't a man be more like a woman?" All of the women in the company thought Julia was wonderful. And we were shocked when Carl showed up at the party with a woman who had brassy blond hair, was very forward, and who bragged that she had "picked Carl up" at the laundromat.

The fact is that Carl is not a particularly deluded man. Men see things differently than women, and it does no good to beat up yourself or the men in your life over the differences. Instead, you have to learn to understand the way men think and then use your understanding to get your message across.

Let's examine some of the major differences in the perceptions of men versus the perceptions of women.

DIFFERENCES IN MALE AND FEMALE PERCEPTIONS

1. Men Deal in Impressions, Not Specifics. Have you ever watched a woman walk into a room full of men and women? The guys look at her quickly, giving her the "once over" and either return to what they were doing before or, if they like what they saw, look her over again, this time writing her into a fantasy.

Women, on the other hand, begin to size up the woman from every angle. Their initial glance takes much longer, since they are analyzing her clothes, her figure, and the look on her face. If we could hear the thoughts of the men, they might be something like this:

"I've never seen her before. Love that hair. She looks like fun. Reminds me of a cheerleader in high school. I can just see her sitting beside me in my convertible, her hair blowing as we drive. . . . I wonder how I can meet her?"

The women, on the other hand, are thinking:

"I bet her hair is bleached. Why did she wear that sweater with that skirt? The colors don't really match. Stylish shoes. I bet she paid a fortune for them. But she really should wear different color hose . . ."

The fact that the woman is wearing fashionable shoes may score points with the other women, but most men in the

cathy®

by Cathy Guisewite

room wouldn't notice if she were barefoot. They're more intrigued with the image she portrays. For women, the image is made up of specifics that they add up to form an impression. Men, however, start with the positive or negative overall image and begin to add or subtract points. That's why the first impression you make on a man is so important. And that brings us to the second point.

2. *Men Seek to Reinforce Their Impressions with Evidence.* Women's minds are not made up as quickly as men's, so they typically reexamine the evidence before they develop a lasting impression. Men, however, form opinions more rapidly and then seek the evidence to support their conclusions.

For example, when the new woman who has entered the room walks up to a man who has already been favorably impressed, she has to do very little to win his heart. He doesn't notice that her sweater doesn't match her skirt since he's already redressed her in a cheerleader's outfit and placed her in the passenger's seat of his convertible. As long as she doesn't destroy the image he's created, she doesn't have to be particularly witty or wonderful.

If, on the other hand, he has already decided that she looks "motherly," she will have to undo that image before she ever begins to accumulate points in her favor. That's why it's critical to understand the image you have with the opposite sex. If you seem motherly, or intimidating, or too young, you will first need to unravel that stereotype in a man's mind before recreating an impression.

If you have learned that people describe you as intimidating, remember that in your first conversation with a man you will need to dispel that image. That doesn't mean you should act like an airhead. Just remember that a man is seeking to reinforce the first image he had. Tell him something unexpected like, "I always feel like a little girl among grown ups when I go to a party like this." He can hardly consider you intimidating when you have painted him a picture of childhood. Explode his image by turning it on him: "I was a bit hesitant to talk to you. You seem so confident and in control." If he says, "Who me? Actually, I was thinking that about you," you know that his stereotype has been undone, and you can move on to create the image you prefer. And your job will be made easier by the next male characteristic we are going to discuss.

3. Men Believe What They Hear. Women tend to suspect that a person is bragging or exaggerating, while most men will accept what they hear as true until proven wrong. This is where the principle "You're as beautiful as you feel" plays a key role. When you feel beautiful, you exude an aura of confidence. And that confidence grows as others sense it and give you positive feedback. If you find ways to tell a man that others find you attractive, he will believe you are attractive unless all evidence contradicts it. That doesn't mean you brag about all of the dates you've had. But it does mean that you never put yourself down; you act like he's a lucky man to be with you; and you hold your head high.

Women tend to think that bragging is one of the worst sins imaginable, so they often play down everything about themselves to men. Then they're surprised when a man believes what they say and never asks them out again. They also find it unbelievable that a woman who "thinks she's hot stuff" does, in fact, get asked out by guys and treated as if she is.

Why do guys want to date women who are considered to be "a catch"? Because dating a woman who others find attractive makes them feel important. And that brings us to my next point.

4. Men Have Strong Egos, but Often Lack Confidence. Women don't understand the fact that guys who seem the most egotistical are the ones most lacking in confidence.

They tend to think that a guy who struts around flexing his muscles needs to be "cut down to size" and are disgusted when he dates a woman who tells him he's wonderful all of the time. Women seem to think that there is a certain amount of praise or ego gratification owed to every man and if you go beyond that, he will be spoiled.

Men are also more susceptible to peer pressure than women and want not just the adoration of the woman they are with, but also the envy of other men. That's part of the reason you may have to overcome "inertia" if you haven't been dating much recently. If guys haven't seen you with another man, they may be afraid to take the bold step of asking you out. What if their buddies don't like you? What if the guys think he's desperate?

Women who are perceived as being a "man's woman" tend to be friendly to most guys and are often seen in the company of men, even ones who are just friends. This tends to make them more desirable to guys who see them being popular with their friends. That's why it's a mistake to never go out with a guy unless you're really interested in him or to turn down a date with a guy when you might be interested in his friend. Most men view rejection of their friends as evidence that you would reject them, too. But if their friends like you, they tend to believe that they will like you, too.

This is really another indication that men lack confidence and rarely trust their own instincts. They need to know that other guys think you are an acceptable choice before they ask you out. They also need to know that you are interested in them. And even though you may think you're sending clear signals, they may be too subtle.

5. Subtlety Is Lost on Most Men. The fear of rejection is an overwhelming factor in most single men's lives. They would rather go out with a less than ideal woman who they know won't reject them than ask out a beautiful woman who might say no. What often amazes me is to watch a woman giving out signals that she is interested in a man and then to later hear him say, "Oh, she's just friendly to everyone." Guys have a difficult time making the first move, even though they think they should be the ones who actually ask a woman out. A woman must make the first move in most cases to show interest and to help the relationship progress from the attention to the attraction stage.

Just saying "hello" won't do it. A woman needs to show a man that she thinks he's special, that she would like to spend time with him, that she can't think of anyone with whom she'd rather be trapped in an elevator. What most women consider to be outrageous flirtation is hardly noticeable to most guys.

I was sitting at dinner one evening with a wonderful single friend of mine who had just confessed to having a crush on a man with whom she worked. A successful professional woman, she could easily discuss a budget or a promotional plan, but she couldn't even think of ways to let this man know she was interested. She seemed to think he would just know about her interest. When I really pushed her to "make a move," she reluctantly replied, "I know you're right. I'll save my pride and he'll end up running off and marrying some cute young thing who falls all over him." My friend is right. Any man is susceptible to obvious praise, even infatuation. If you're interested in a man, show him—or take the chance of losing him to a woman who will.

Perhaps it sounds like I am stereotyping men. But read a book by a man about men: *Understanding the Man in Your Life* by Norman Wright (Word, 1987). This book draws the lines even more sharply between the way men and women think and how that is reflected in their behavior. If you want to meet and marry Mr. Right, you need to know how he thinks. (Believe me, it's even more important to understand this after you marry him!)

Using your notebook, list the behaviors that confuse or frustrate you about men. Then give yourself the homework assignment of reading more about how men think. Or better yet, sit down with a male friend and ask him to help you understand why men act the way they do. After I spent time interviewing several men, I came up with five areas of concern which I will explore in the next chapter. Rather than making me feel more confused about how men think, I found that my research showed me how much I could identify with some of the struggles men have. And I learned some valuable techniques for defusing some of the conventional weapons we use in the war between the sexes.

CHAPTER NINE

♥

Music to
His Ears

I just don't understand what's going on with Bill," said Janet one day. "He seems to like me. I really am attracted to him. But he just doesn't ask me out.

"Last week we were both working late. As we were leaving the office, he asked me if I had any plans for the evening. When I said no, I naturally expected that he'd ask me to join him for dinner. Instead he said, 'Neither do I.' Then he said good-bye and walked to his car.

"Why doesn't he ask me out?"

Janet was dealing with many of the factors we discussed in the last chapter. But she hadn't learned to apply practical solutions to these problems, and she was in danger of losing Bill's attention.

A friend of mine once observed, "I'll never understand how men think. All I can do is study them and apply what I've learned, just like I did in school. It's like learning chemical formulas and then applying them. They just work. That's how it is with men. Certain approaches bring almost predictable responses."

My friend might have been simplifying the situation a bit, but she's right in a way. Women probably can't fully understand how men think. But there are some basic needs men have and some basic ways women can help meet those needs. In interviewing dozens of men for this book, I discovered five statements of needs that men expressed over and over again in different ways. I also asked the men to give me ways that women have helped meet these needs.

The answers to that question tended to be fairly predictable, too. By following these guidelines, most women should be able to respond in the "right" ways to men, even if they don't fully understand those needs.

When women think about men's needs, they often wonder about sex. It is true that most men tend to be more sexual in nature than most women. Some of this is biological; some of it may be sociological. Men encourage each other to joke about sex. To some men, intimacy is equated with sex. But many men try to satisfy their deeper psychological needs through sex and are still disappointed. That's why a woman who does not sleep with a man, but does fulfill him psychologically, can keep a man satisfied in a relationship. On the other hand, there are women who do not have high moral standards, but still can't maintain a relationship. Don't be fooled into believing that men's needs can only be satisfied sexually. Their needs are much more complex than that. To help you understand them better, let's look at five needs they most often express.

FIVE NEEDS MEN MOST OFTEN EXPRESS

1. "I Need Someone to Make Me Feel Important." If there is one thing you could do to endear yourself to every man you come in contact with for the rest of your life, it would be to make him feel important. Actually, both men and women have this need and those who learn to fulfill it in others often go on to accomplish great things themselves.

Think about ways that other people make you feel important. Chances are, they find ways to make you feel special—they make you feel heads above the rest. They do this in simple ways as well as more complex ones. It's not something that comes naturally to most people. Our natural tendencies lead us to find ways to focus on ourselves instead of others. So making men feel important requires discipline and practice. Start with the simple things.

Say his name. Everyone loves to hear his or her name. As you talk to a man, use his name occasionally in the conversation. If you're in a group, say something like, "Rob, what do you think about that?" When you pass him in the hall, don't just say hello, say, "Hi, Rob."

Listen for clues as to what he prefers to be called. For example, some men are often called by their nickname but introduce themselves by their full name. Try using his full name and see how he responds. Ask him if he minds if you call him Richard instead of Dick. Many men prefer the more formal sound of their full name, but have been using their nickname since school and can't break others of the habit. By taking the time to find out what he prefers, you show that you think he's special. And if you are the only one calling him by his preferred name, you can bet he'll think you're special, too.

Look him in the eye. It's amazing how many times you talk to someone without really looking him in the eye. Remind yourself to look into his eyes when he is talking to you so that he feels you are really listening to what he is saying. It doesn't hurt to even comment on the color of his eyes. Once again, by noticing, you've let him know that you think he's special.

It's often more difficult to look into someone else's eyes when you are doing the talking. But by doing so, you will see his reactions, almost before he registers them himself. Another interesting aspect of looking at someone else while you are talking is that you can't go on and on and bore your companion without knowing it. A person who is bored will stop looking at you. That means it's time to stop talking and turn the spotlight back on him.

Be appreciative. Notice everything you can about a man and find ways to praise him. If he holds a door open for you, thank him. Many men are afraid that showing common courtesies may be perceived as being chauvinistic. Yet many women complain that guys don't treat them very well. If you want a guy to treat you courteously, thank him any time he shows the smallest inclination toward courtesy. Don't expect it, and don't take it for granted. After all, any man who opens the door for you has had to think about it and go out of his way. A word of thanks is more than appropriate.

Besides saying thank you, find ways to state what you really like about him. If he is the kind of person who always shows up on time, tell him you appreciate timeliness and think he's considerate to plan ahead so that he arrives on time. If he wears nice ties to work, tell him you think he has the best taste in ties of anyone in the office.

Find out what he likes about himself. We all think that we're special in certain ways, and we think those who appreciate us in those ways are particularly perceptive. If you want a man to really feel important, find out what he likes about himself, then help reinforce that view. No, it's not too bold to simply ask him what he thinks he does best or how he'd like to live his life if he could do anything. Ask him what he's most proud of accomplishing. Be direct and interested. Let him know that what he thinks is important to you.

Now let's consider another need men often express.

2. *"I Need to Know That She Likes Me."* Most men I interviewed said they wouldn't ask a girl out unless they were pretty sure she was going to say yes. By asking more questions, I discovered that to most guys "pretty sure" meant 99 percent sure. Women sometimes have a hard time understanding or accepting this. They often feel that they shouldn't ask a guy out (that's probably true, especially with more conservative men), but they wonder why their "hints" aren't understood.

For example, in the case of Janet and Bill, she thought it would be obvious to Bill that she would like to join him for dinner. But Bill hadn't received enough positive feedback to feel totally sure he wouldn't be rejected. Furthermore, he wasn't willing to take the big leap of asking Janet to dinner after she had said "nothing." Believe it or not, he heard that as potential for a major rejection. Had she refused his offer of dinner, he would have felt that she was rejecting *him*, not just the invitation.

What should Janet have done differently? First, she should have been working on letting Bill know she thought he was special. She probably needed to be more obvious. Second, she could have played out the encounter quite differently. Let's look at some possibilities.

Initiate. Calling up a guy and asking him out for a formal date might be more than some guys could handle. But asking a guy to join you on the "spur of the moment" for dinner is not too pushy. The trick is to think it all through first. Janet had planned to work late in order to catch Bill alone. But she hadn't thought about what exactly might happen.

She should have been the first to initiate the contact. For example:

Janet: *"I'm starving."*
Bill: *"Me, too."*
Janet: *"I hear they have dinner specials at the new restaurant down the street."*

At this point it's an easy leap for Bill to say, "That sounds great. Do you want to go?" But if he simply says, "That sounds great," it's perfectly acceptable for Janet to say, "I hate to eat alone. Want to join me?"

If Bill has something else to do, he can easily say, "Not tonight," and neither Janet nor Bill have suffered a major rejection. Furthermore, Janet will have let Bill know that she'd like to have dinner with him sometime, and it will be much easier for him to ask her out at another point. Many men need to have an obvious indication which they can think about for a while before making their own move.

The conversation that actually transpired between Janet and Bill left both of them unhappy. Janet wondered what was wrong with Bill for not asking her out and the next day acted distant toward him and somewhat defensive. Bill, on the other hand, probably drove home telling himself that he was a dope for not asking her out, but then thought of all the reasons why she might have rejected him.

Janet hadn't planned far enough ahead when she imagined her encounter with Bill. But, of course, it's not easy to plan every circumstance in which you find yourself in contact with a man you'd like to spend more time with. One of the easiest ways to initiate time together is to relate it to the weather. For example:

"What a beautiful evening. I feel like going for a walk, but I'm a bit afraid of going alone. Would you like to walk with me?"

"Wow, it's really getting icy. Would you mind walking me to my car?"

"It's beginning to rain. Want to share my umbrella?"

Remember to always lessen the risk of rejection in any situation. Even if you are the initiator, you don't want to be rejected. Make the request casual but specific, and don't be afraid to let a man know that you're asking him because you would enjoy his company.

Get someone else involved. Basically, this is the matchmaker approach to dating and can be somewhat risky. You may have used it quite crudely but effectively in junior high school, but it becomes more difficult as you become an adult.

If you are attracted to a guy, especially one you see regularly, try to find an intermediary to help you out. A married man or woman can be a great help here because there's less chance of the person in the middle getting caught up in either person's emotions.

Don't involve the whole office in your crush or tell people you hardly know. But if you have a trusted friend, confess your feelings and see if that person knows the man at all. If your friend knows him, hint that you wish you knew if he were dating or interested in someone else.

A riskier approach is to befriend someone close to the man to whom you are attracted. You have to be both subtle and direct, and you could be walking into a minefield, but at least you can get your message across fairly quickly.

Be direct. Not every woman can pull this off, but there's nothing wrong with going up to a guy and saying, "You look like an interesting person. I'd like to get to know you." Or if you already know a guy, simply say something like, "You know, I'd rather talk to you than just about anyone else in this company." Or, "I think you are one of my favorite people." Or simply, "I really like you."

Sure, it takes courage. But there's nothing immoral, unethical, or rude about letting someone know how you feel. Even if a guy isn't interested in you, you'll probably make his day.

I tried this technique once at a big party where I hardly knew anyone. I hadn't been introduced to this man, but I went up to him and told him that he had great eyebrows. He laughingly told me that he'd always thought they were too big, so he was glad someone liked them. We went on to discuss other things, but it was a great ice breaker.

Next time you want to let a man know you like him, remember, you can initiate an invitation, get someone else involved, or be direct. Now let's look at a third need men most often expressed in my interviews.

3. "I Need Someone to Help Me Feel Like a Winner." Almost every man I know is basically competitive. But because guys compete, especially athletically, from an early age, they are painfully aware that they don't always win. "For many men, winning is tied to their identity," says Norman Wright in *Understanding the Man in Your Life.* "It is their way of proving their masculine power."

Let him catch you. As I pointed out in the last chapter, men are always aware of what other men think. They want men to be envious of their date. They want to know that you are a "catch." Some women have a knack for seeming desirable. Others have to work at it.

Be sure you are approachable, but not too available. Don't be waiting after work every night for the guy you want to bump into. Dress up some days and hurry off after work so that he thinks you have other men waiting for you. You don't have to lie to anyone. Just be friendly but busy so that he feels he must compete for you.

As we discussed in the chapter on approachability, learn to have a certain air of mystery about you. Show up slightly late for a party. Don't always be ready to join the gang after work. Don't tell everyone what you do every evening or on the weekend.

If a guy does begin to show interest, be friendly but go slowly. When I learned to fish as a young girl, I was taught that patience was more important after a fish began to nibble than at any other time. One had to use a very subtle movement to keep the fish interested because it was easily scared away just before it took the hook and could be reeled in. So it is with many men. They may be on the verge of falling hard for you, but they can also be scared off quite easily if you show too much interest or not enough mystery. The essentially competitive nature of a man leads him to think, "This is too easy. Maybe she's not such a catch after all."

Give him a blue ribbon. Some men are more competitive than others, of course, and once you've made a man feel special, you may want to go even further. If he seems to really enjoy the techniques you used to make him feel important, try finding ways to compare him favorably with others.

For example, if he is a man in your office, you might want to say, "I really think you are the best salesman in the company" or something along those lines. If you've met him at church, comment on how much more perceptive he is than others or how much more he's thought through his beliefs than other men you've met. Ask him for his opinion on something, such as a car you're thinking of buying or a stereo system. Tell him he seems to know more about cars or stereos than anyone else you know.

The important thing to remember here is to compare him to others. Find a way that he stands out, then push the comparison to the point that you basically say, "You are the clear winner in this area."

Of course, you should base your comparison on some supporting evidence, but don't be too literal. We all think we're smarter or better or more perceptive in some areas of life. The trick is to find an area where he is at least above average. Then compare him favorably with others in an effort to show that if you were judging, he'd clearly get the blue ribbon.

Some women balk at this type of flattery because they are afraid it is obviously false. Try it on any man you know and see how he responds. Most guys will say something like, "Oh, come on. You don't really mean it." But if you persist, almost every man will move to "You really think so?" and will stand a little taller and look at you with new appreciation. Think about how you feel when someone praises you —even if it's obvious flattery. Chances are you feel great. Why not give that same gift to someone else?

Now we come to a fourth need men express.

4. "I Need Someone Who Will Let Me Be Myself." Every man—just like every woman—is a unique creature with assets and flaws, strengths and weaknesses. By the time most of us reach our early twenties, we begin to come to terms with our uniqueness. We change what we can, but most of us will never fit society's ideal, so we learn to find others who help reinforce who we are.

One of the biggest mistakes single women make is finding a man and then deciding to change him into their ideal. True, I have seen many relationships where the love and support of a woman have actually transformed a man and helped him grow and flourish. But I have also seen women criticize and complain until a guy is either beaten down or simply has had enough and leaves.

Never criticize. There is simply nothing more devastating to a man (or to a woman, although she is more able to handle it) than criticism. Criticize a man, even "for his own good," and you will have undermined his confidence. Some women think this is good because it makes a man more humble. But, in fact, it simply breaks the spirit of a man and causes him to be passive. Passivity is one of the greatest complaints women have about men, yet they have often beaten a man down until he has no choice but to "go with the flow" instead of initiating action.

Some women don't even recognize that they are being critical. Women who are in responsible positions at work often have a hard time turning off their critical skills during off hours. A woman manager, for example, is paid to be a trouble shooter at the office. But when she goes on a date and suggests a more direct route to the theater than her date is taking, or finds reasons why the suggested plan for the evening is inefficient, she is criticizing.

I'm always amazed by women who see this as an issue of equality and feminism instead of good manners and common courtesy. Just because you might be right doesn't make your actions correct. If a man has taken the time to plan a date and you begin reorchestrating it in your own way, you have crossed into simple critical behavior. Isn't it more important to show a man that you think he's special than to get to the theater earlier? His way of doing things might not be exactly the way you would do them, but criticizing him will rarely change him into your ideal man, and will generally lead him to find a more positive date next time.

Several men I interviewed said that they preferred to date younger women because they "didn't demand as much." When I asked for examples, it became quite clear that what they were really saying was that younger women were less critical.

Don't ridicule. Some women think they are being flirtatious by laughing at a guy or "putting him down." Some guys do respond to this type of flirtation. But most guys are scared off and really hurt by a woman who teases too much or ridicules, even in jest.

If you have fallen into this type of habit, break yourself of it. It tends to come from your own insecurity and only feeds on a man's insecurity. If you want to start an honest, meaningful relationship with a man, don't tease him in a negative way.

However, you need to be aware that some guys use negative teasing when they are beginning to find themselves attracted to a woman. It's a way of showing attention without putting themselves on the line. If a guy does this to you, do not throw the barbs back in his direction. Turn his criticism of you back on yourself, and you'll find him running to your defense and moving to a deeper level of understanding. Take, for example, the following scenario:

Henry: "Joanie thinks she's got such great legs that she's wearing a miniskirt."

Joanie might be tempted to say, "Well, look at you. You'd think someone wearing a shirt that tight would at least have some muscles to show off."

The exchange would escalate into joking and not-so-joking insults. Instead, Joanie could say, "Actually, I just threw my long skirt into the washing machine and it shrunk. I was hoping no one would notice."

It's an easy leap for Henry to turn the conversation back to a positive course by saying, "I think everyone will notice. Maybe you could throw all of your long skirts into the washer in the future."

The second exchange establishes the fact that Henry thinks Joanie is attractive, and they both leave the conversation feeling good about themselves and each other. But the first exchange pokes at some vulnerabilities that few of us can afford to dismiss. Joanie walks away wondering if she should have worn a longer skirt, and Henry becomes self-conscious about his physique. They're not sure what they think of each other or themselves.

Develop trust. The ideal relationship allows us to be ourselves in front of the other person without fear of rejection. Find ways to foster trust in your relationship with a man, and you will discover that your relationship grows very naturally. Encourage him to confide in you. Never repeat what a man has told you.

When a man gets to the point that he is able to openly admit his faults to you, you know that he trusts you. Realize that he is giving you power over him and use it very carefully. Never use that knowledge against him or point out his faults in front of others. Instead, make him believe that you are on his side through your actions and your attitude.

It is often difficult for men to place their trust in others, especially in women. But once a man does trust you, you are well on your way to developing a lasting relationship.

Finally, we come to the fifth need most often expressed by the men I interviewed.

5. *"I Need Someone to Help Me Feel Strong."* Despite the elevation of "the sensitive man," men still feel a need to be strong in most situations—physically, emotionally, and even spiritually. Of course, a man does not always feel strong. But he hardly ever feels able to admit that and worries about his very identity when he begins to see weaknesses in himself.

The world in which we live tends to elevate the strengths of women, simply because we were characterized as "the weaker sex" for so long. Frankly, I think life was easier for men and women when that stereotype was widely accepted. I'm not saying it was right, nor am I saying that women are weaker than men. What I am saying is that men still have a greater need to feel strong than women do. Because they are competitive, they have to feel stronger than others. Feeling stronger than women gives them the opportunity to both excel and act as protector, a role they are often more able to play simply because of their physical strength.

Many men I interviewed were willing to honestly admit how scared they were of strong women. They were not male chauvinists or wimps; they were simply average guys who were afraid that they weren't strong enough to satisfy the demands of women who wanted them to initiate dates, but not dominate; be courteous and chivalrous, but not

cathy®

by Cathy Guisewite

chauvinistic; lead the family, but at the same time encourage their wives to excel. After several interviews, I began to feel the incredible pressure many men are under.

Single women, on the other hand, are quick to complain that guys don't take the lead in a relationship, don't plan out dates, don't act courteously, and aren't spiritual leaders. It seems that many women want the idealized old-fashioned guy, but expect him to be liberated at the right moments.

Reality is that society in general, and most women in particular, ask that a man be strong and even dominant. Most men don't feel totally up to this vague challenge, but do their best to walk through the minefield, knowing that to go too much one way could lead them to be called a male chauvinist pig, yet to go the other direction means potential challenges to their masculinity. Women can ease the pressure on men in this area by helping them feel strong.

Don't ask too much. So many women have very high expectations for men. They've seen the movies in which the leading man always shows courage and confidence. Real men aren't like that any more than real women all look like Kathleen Turner. So what if a guy wears casual clothes for a formal party or acts tongue-tied on your first date? No one is perfect, and everyone deserves another chance.

One of the first times I met the man I eventually married, he was wearing blue jeans that were too short. At that point in time, everyone's jeans dragged on the floor if they were "cool," and Bob's jeans definitely were not cool. If I'd judged him solely on his appearance that day, I might have missed out on a man who happens to dress impeccably for work and formal situations and wears the first comfortable thing he can find on weekends. My ideal man might have never worn jeans that were too short, but then Bob's ideal woman probably never wore a worn-out, terry bathrobe like my favorite lounging outfit.

Tell him he's strong. A man's own name may be music to his ears, but hearing that he's strong feeds his psyche. The old caricature of a woman feeling a man's muscles and telling him what a man he is may seem silly, but there's some truth to be learned from it. A man needs to hear that he is strong because he equates it with masculinity. Tell him, very obviously, that you admire his strength in certain areas (physically, emotionally, intellectually, spiritually). Use words like *strong, secure, brave,* and *powerful* to describe him.

Let him protect you. Most women admit that they like it when a guy is protective. Yet so many women have a hard time playing to the protective instincts of a man. Learn to ask for his help if you want him to protect you. Stop being so independent and admit that it's nice to have someone to lean on at times.

Instead of walking to your car alone, ask a guy to walk with you. Instead of carrying heavy boxes up the stairs, ask a man if he'd mind helping you out. Once again, don't expect help and thank him sincerely for going out of his way. But remember that men are stronger than women in many ways, and there's nothing wrong with acknowledging that strength and appreciating it.

You don't have to underplay your own strength or act helpless in order to make a man feel strong. But if you always refuse help or act independent, only the most confident man will be able to crack through the barriers you create. We all need help at different times, and learning to ask for it is the sign of a healthy person who acknowledges that she can have a meaningful relationship with another human being.

CHAPTER TEN

Where Have All the Good Men Gone?

We're looking for a few good men" the Army recruiting poster proclaims, and that could be the battle cry of many single women, too. Where are all of the single guys? Did they just disappear after a certain age?

Many women feel surprised to leave college, where they dated often, and find themselves in the working world without a date for months or even years. Sure, they meet men. But most are married and surprisingly few are like the guys they easily met and dated in college.

Becoming part of the adult world of rent and car payments and health insurance is a shock to most of us who have lived with parents and then in the semireality of college. But even more shocking is the realization that we will never again be with so many people who are like us in so many ways. Even finding female friends who share our values and background can be difficult. But meeting eligible men can seem almost impossible at times.

The fact is that after you leave college, your ability to meet men diminishes dramatically. No longer can you go out for a stroll across campus or take a study break at the snack bar and meet someone. Instead of being a natural, daily occurrence, meeting men becomes a job.

The older you are, the more of a full-time job finding an eligible and compatible man becomes. You have to work hard to find opportunities to meet men. Every day counts.

cathy®

by Cathy Guisewite

This is not meant to depress you. Instead, you need to put yourself into training—dating boot camp—and get serious about meeting men or you will become lazy. Time after time, I've talked to single women who complain that they don't date. When I've asked them what they're doing about meeting men, they give me vague answers about going to the church singles group or standing around the coffee pot at work. If that's your attitude, you might as well buy a stack of romance novels and escape into fantasy land.

Meeting men takes work. And just reading the list of places to meet men will not bring you any closer to a man unless you do something about it. You need to make a specific attempt to meet men *each and every day.*

Remember to keep adding to your lists of "prospects" in your notebook, especially as men you already know come to mind. The men you will meet in the places listed in these next two chapters are new men, but you should never concentrate on them to the exclusion of the guys you already know.

A friend of mine named Sandy was trying out some of the places mentioned in the next two chapters when she was reminded of an old friend from college. She reestablished contact with him through mutual friends and began seeing him again. She still dated other men and found trying out some of the new places was really fun. But the more she dated other men, the more she realized how much she cared for her college friend. In the meantime, she had fun meeting different kinds of people before she decided to "settle down" with Mr. Right.

The places listed here take into account both quantity of men and quality of men. Singles bars and personal ads in newspapers may bring you quantity, but I have doubts about the quality of men you'll find. If you are specifically looking for a man who shares your faith, you should keep in mind that the five places we will be discussing in this chapter give you an opportunity to self-select a man since you can get to know something about him. The more general ways of meeting men, which we will discuss in the next chapter, often mean that you will have to go out with a guy before you have any sense of his values.

Remember the 80/20 rule as you look for men: 80 percent of dates come from 20 percent of the places you meet guys. The following five places are where you can most reasonably expect to meet guys. You should remember to concentrate your efforts on these before moving along to the next chapter.

1. Your job. You spend more time at work than at any other place, so naturally, this is the best place to meet men. If you aren't totally settled on a specific career, follow these guidelines:

Look into a field dominated by men. If you've got the brains, go for medicine, law, or accounting. Many businesses are traditionally male-dominated for no reason other than the fact that men happened to be there first. Check out various industries to discover where men are concentrated. Work as a temporary for a while, or take a job with UPS or another delivery service which will expose you to many businesses and fields.

Go to work for the largest employer you can find. The simple fact is that you are going to meet more people in a major corporation employing hundreds than in a small office with less than a dozen people.

Look for a company that has many new positions, or one which requires sales people to call often. Some industries are static, where others are growing and bringing in more people and services daily. The more new faces, the greater your chances of meeting someone.

Don't be afraid to change jobs. Early in your career is an important time to look into various fields. Although sticking with a job for less than a year is not a good signal to future employers, if you are willing to say that you discovered that your opportunities were limited, or that you did not really like the job, most prospective employers will not hold it against you.

Once you do settle into a job, remember to put your best foot forward each and every day. You never can tell who will walk into your office. Just because you decide that there aren't any prospects at work, don't fail to dress each day as if you were planning to meet the man of your dreams, and don't forget to walk into your office with a smile on your face. New people come into offices every day. Furthermore, each married person at the office probably has some single friends. If you are a pleasant person at the office and are fun to be with, your married friends will probably begin looking for guys to "set you up with."

When I first moved to a new city, nearly all of my co-workers were married. After a few weeks, they discovered that I didn't know anyone in town, and one by one they began inviting me over for dinner or parties where they conveniently arranged to have an eligible man present. True, it seemed a bit awkward at times, but I did meet men that way and even began to date one or two of the men that my friends had set me up with.

Whatever the field you're in, for the sake of your personal as well as your professional future, make it a point to pursue any avenues of education or development open to you. Join clubs in your field, such as graphic arts clubs, advertising clubs, health care professional clubs, etc. Attend annual conventions and training seminars. Your boss will be pleased, and you'll be surprised by the number of people you meet.

2. Church. When I interviewed single men who wanted to meet a woman who shared their faith and values, the first place they said they looked for a mate was at church. When I ask happy young couples where they met each other, church is one of the more common answers, even for people who don't consider themselves to be religious.

Single women often complain that they see the same old guys at church, yet it's important to remember that church really is a great place to meet guys if you work at it. First, just like your place of employment, you will have more opportunities if you choose a church with many members. Choose the largest church of the denomination with which you feel comfortable and attend every service for a month. That's right. Go to Sunday school, church, Sunday evening service, midweek service, and every other meeting offered. After a month you should have a fairly good idea about the friendliness of the church, how comfortable you feel, and if there are enough single people in the church to give you a chance of meeting people. If you feel that this is the right church, stay there; but if you have doubts, try another church for another month.

Don't be afraid to try different denominations, even if you're afraid that you'll feel out of place. If you grew up as a Methodist, you might be surprised to discover many of the same hymns are sung in some Lutheran churches. Or if you grew up as a Baptist, you might welcome the liturgy of an Episcopal church for a change. Don't be too set in your ways. Try as many different churches as you can feel comfortable in. Even if you settle on a church, perhaps once a month you should attend a service at a different church, just to meet new people.

When you do go to church, arrive early and plan to linger after the service. Introduce yourself to the people who sit next to you—don't wait for them to introduce themselves. Offer to help in any way possible that will give you visibility and/or the opportunity to see most people arriving. If you play the piano and your church needs a pianist to fill in, by all means volunteer. Singing in the choir gives you a great view of the congregation, too, and helps you meet others. Some churches need greeters to welcome people at the doors.

If you travel on business, try to schedule out-of-town meetings on a Monday or a Friday, then stay over the weekend in the city and attend one of the largest churches in that town. Keep circulating among churches as much as possible, and when you are in a church, do whatever you can to meet people. Always attend the singles Sunday school class, and be sure to stay for the coffee hour between services. If you feel awkward, smile, introduce yourself to the person next to you, and tell people that you're new. Most people will try to help you out and will introduce you to others. So what if you feel a bit uncomfortable at first? Remember that you will never find a better place to meet a man who shares your dreams and values.

3. Friends. The third best way to meet men is through friends because they care about you, can prescreen guys, and can arrange ways for you to meet. Married friends are often a big help here, especially if you let them know that you aren't dating anyone seriously and are open to their efforts to set you up. Some friends won't want to make assumptions about your private life, so a good way to let it be known that you are looking for someone is to ask your married friends how they met their spouses. If they don't take the hint, say something like, "It's really hard to meet nice guys in this town." Don't go on and on about not dating or say anything that in any way indicates desperation. No one wants to set up a friend with a desperate woman.

Single friends can be a good source of dates, too. Cultivate friendships with guys, even if you aren't interested in them romantically. Don't play games with them; let them know that you are "just friends." You might even want to purposely befriend guys who are younger, or so different from you that most people understand your friendship is nothing romantic. Most guys have several other close male friends whom you will eventually meet. Even if you don't become romantically involved with your male friends or their friends, they can give you invaluable insights into the working of the male mind. They can also help you learn where guys go for fun and what they are looking for in a woman.

Women friends can sometimes introduce you to eligible men, although this can be tricky. Many a woman has introduced a girlfriend to a guy whom she describes as "just a friend," only to get very upset if the two begin to date. Be sure you don't get involved in a messy triangle if a woman friend introduces you to a guy.

One young woman told me about a party that single women gave in which each woman invited four single men, preferably guys that she wasn't interested in, but thought her friends might enjoy. Called a "new blood" party, the idea was to form an informal network of people who might begin to date. Try it yourself, especially if you start with a large enough group to make it fun and interesting.

4. Part-time job. One of the most overlooked ways of meeting guys is a part-time job. Even if you work full time in an office, consider working one or two evenings a week or Saturdays in the men's department of a clothing store, or in a sporting goods store, or bookstore. The times you are working are exactly when guys who work in an office are shopping, and you'll meet a whole new group of people.

Try being a waitress at a restaurant where young single people often go, or even consider working as a checker in a grocery store during evenings or Saturdays. Maybe it sounds boring, but you'll meet people and earn extra money. And besides, you don't have to do it forever. Just try it for a while. Most stores need extra help during the Christmas holiday season, or during a major sale.

When you are working, especially in a job where you meet people constantly, remember to concentrate on being approachable. Smile, smile, smile. Be genuinely helpful. If possible, wear something that invites comments, like a fun pin, or interesting earrings, or colorful scarf. Ask "How are you today?" and welcome conversation (as long as it doesn't take you away from your work). Even if you're helping a married woman, you'll be surprised at the benefits. Not only will your cheerfulness help your outlook on life, but, once again, people will begin to introduce you to others.

When I worked in a department store, I helped an older woman one day who was having a difficult time selecting some Christmas gifts for relatives. About a week later, she returned to the store with her handsome grandson in tow. She insisted that we meet, since "we both seemed like such nice young people."

If you are specifically looking for a conservative Christian man, go to work in a Christian bookstore. Although it's true that more women than men go to Christian bookstores, many have sons or brothers or grandsons whom they would love to "fix up" with a nice Christian woman. Be outgoing, friendly, and helpful. Your efforts will be appreciated and some of the people you meet will become allies in your dating efforts.

5. *School.* If you have been out of college for a few years and still haven't met someone, consider returning to graduate school. The best places to meet single men are medical school, law school, seminary, and business school. If you aren't willing to make the commitment to a full-fledged graduate program, see if you can audit a class.

If a graduate degree is beyond your interest, budget, or abilities, then sign up for classes through the continuing education division of your county, YMCA, local college, museum, or library. Take classes in subjects that would especially attract men, such as finance and investments, sports, architecture, science, or law. If there is a seminary nearby, try to take classes in biblical studies, rather than counseling or church education, where classes are often dominated by women.

Having this list is a start, but you have to take the initiative. Under the strategy section in your notebook, list two action items relating to the places in this chapter. Here are some suggestions:

1. Attend the annual convention of my company's trade association.

2. Consider changing jobs to work in a larger office.

3. Work as a temporary for the next six months to see what jobs are available and to meet new people.

4. Ask my boss about training opportunities available to me.

5. Attend a different church next Sunday.

6. Attend a church in a nearby town.

7. Plan to attend a new church during my vacation or on my next business trip.

8. Volunteer to help in my church or begin to sing in the choir.

9. Ask my married friends how they met and try their suggestions.

10. Let friends know that I'm available.

11. Get a part-time job in a sporting goods store, men's clothing store, or bookstore.

12. Take one evening class during the next three months.

13. Get catalogs from graduate schools and seminaries.

14. Find out if my company gives assistance to employees who attend school.

15. Get a list of the free lectures offered at the library or local museums.

If you begin today, three months from now you will have met several new men. And chances are at least one of them will be someone you will enjoy getting to know even better.

♥

CHAPTER ELEVEN

More Ways to Meet Men

Take a moment to review last week. What did you do? Besides the forty or more hours spent at work, where did the rest of your time go? How many new people did you meet? If your answer is "none," take a hard look at your lifestyle. Realize that even if there are only two people in your office and no single men in your church, you still have the ability to meet many new people each and every week.

In this chapter, we'll emphasize ways of bringing you in contact with new people. The emphasis, of course, is on single men, but that's not the only point of this exercise. Every new person you meet has something to teach you; he or she will help you stretch and grow. That person has friends and interests that are new to you. Each person you meet represents an opportunity to explore a whole new world.

As you go about your search for Mr. Right, be open to all of the people you will meet. A friend of mine named Sally met an older woman on a bus ride to work. When the woman invited her over for tea one day, she hesitated, but decided it would probably be a nice thing to do for the lonely woman. When she went to the woman's apartment, she was surprised to find that the woman lived in a beautiful condominium full of furniture and artifacts from all over the world. Her late husband had been in the foreign service, and the woman turned out to be a fascinating source of information about far-off lands.

Furthermore, she wasn't lonely at all. She had many friends—young and old—whom she introduced to Sally. Sally became so caught up in the excitement of the people she met that she eventually took the foreign service exam herself, joined the State Department, and married another foreign service officer—all because Sally took the time to have tea with a "lonely old woman" on her bus.

In order to make the most of this chapter, promise yourself three things:

1. I will make an effort to become more aware and more interested in the people around me.

2. I will have a positive attitude about meeting people, even if they aren't attractive single men.

3. I will schedule at least one new activity in every two-week period, specifically as a way to meet new people.

If you want to be sure that you actually follow through, you may want to follow Janet's system. In her notebook she wrote the months of the year down one side of a page, skipping four or five lines in between each entry. She then "scheduled" possible outings by the time of the year.

As you read this chapter, note ideas for activities that appeal to you and begin to schedule them in by the month. Later, take out your calendar and actually schedule specific times for these activities. View them as a commitment you've made, just as anything else that you would note on your calendar. That will keep you from "meaning to get around" to meeting people, and it will help you actually get going.

Ready to begin your adventure? Here are twenty ways to help you meet people.

TWENTY WAYS TO MEET NEW PEOPLE

1. Read the Newspaper. It's a great source of information on special events, visiting speakers, local people, and conferences in your area. Each morning pick up the paper and read it with an eye toward finding new places to explore or activities to attend. Watch especially for:

> Art and craft shows
> Auctions
> Boat and car shows
> Conventions and conferences
> Free lectures
> Gallery openings
> Political rallies or activities
> Visiting speakers at area churches

If you read about someone who inspires you or who seems especially interesting, drop him or her a note and ask if you could buy the person a cup of coffee or lunch. You'd be surprised by the people who will gladly meet you if you show a sincere interest in them.

2. Take Public Transportation Everywhere. Most good-size towns have some form of public transportation. Learn the system and begin to take a bus to work or the train into town. Maybe it's not as fast as driving your own car to work, but who do you meet while sitting alone in your car in bumper-to-bumper traffic?

You don't want to ride the subway in New York alone late at night, but most public transportation is perfectly safe, especially during rush hours or from suburban locations into a city. If you ride the same route at the same time each day, you'll begin to see the "regulars." Some people even begin to sit in the same place each day. After a while, you'll develop a sort of camaraderie with the other people, and you may even get to know each other.

If you are specifically interested in attracting a Christian man, read a C. S. Lewis book as you commute. When I took buses to work, I was amazed at the number of people who felt free to ask me about the book or magazine I was reading at the time. During that phase of my life, I was in graduate school studying business, and I found that men were especially interested when they saw me reading an economics textbook. Think about the type of people you want to meet when you choose your reading material.

3. Take Up Walking. Make it your hobby to walk to as many places as possible. Take up walking as a sport and walk before work. Take a walk during your lunch hour. Get outside whenever you can and walk to as many different places as you can. Don't wear headphones. No one will feel free to talk to you if they have to get your attention and interrupt your listening. Learn to walk purposefully but not too quickly. Smile at people as you pass them or say hello. If you're walking in the morning or on a jogging trail, it's appropriate to say hello, smile, or wave to anyone you pass. There's a certain *esprit de corps* that comes from being out exercising.

When you are walking, always wear a t-shirt or sweat-shirt that says something about you. If you want to specifi-cally attract a Christian man, wear a Young Life shirt or one from a well-known Christian college. Wear a shirt that bears the name of your alma mater, a favorite hobby, or a vacation site. After walking past the same people for a few weeks, you'll discover quite a bit about them from what they wear, and they'll discover something about you.

I was out jogging one day when a man passed me, then turned around and began to run beside me. "When did you graduate?" he asked breathlessly. I was confused until I realized that he had noticed the sweatshirt I was wearing that actually bore the name of an old boyfriend's school! I've had other people smile and remark about a t-shirt I have from a favorite vacation spot in Hawaii. A logo or slogan is an easy way for almost anyone to start a conversation. Try it yourself the next time you see someone wearing a shirt that has some identification on it.

4. *Join a Health Club.* Although some women feel uncomfortable working out with men around, health clubs are still a safe way to meet men. It's easy to strike up a conversation by asking how to use the equipment. (This has little to do with being a "helpless woman." Even though I go to the health club often, I have to ask someone almost every time myself!) And even if you don't meet someone, you'll be improving the way you look and feel.

Be careful about what you wear to a health club. Even modest leotards seem revealing or sexy when you use certain types of equipment. It's perfectly appropriate to wear a baggy t-shirt over a leotard—and then you can wear something that hints at your interests or serves as a conversation starter. In a health club, especially, I would advise wearing something that indicates your values. If you aren't wearing a t-shirt, wear a fish symbol or cross necklace. A Christian guy will probably recognize the symbol and feel more free to talk to you.

Remember that if a man is in a health club, you know little about him except that he can pay the fee and that he's interested in working out. If you meet someone who seems nice, find out if he comes to the club at a regular time. If you're embarrassed to ask him the question directly, say something like, "Is it always so busy as this time of day?" He'll have to indicate something about when he comes when he answers the question.

After you've seen him a few times, it's fine to accept an invitation to have a cup of coffee or for some other casual outing, but remember that you need to use the time to get to know him and learn what he values. Health clubs are only one step away from single bars when it comes to offering the chance to meet people without knowing anything about their values.

5. Take Up Photography. Most photography classes have more guys than women and offer a great opportunity to really get to know people through the subjects of their photos. Even if you've never used more than an Instamatic camera, you can learn to enjoy photography. Just the education process will put you in touch with many men.

Start by going to a photography equipment store. The more specialized, the better chance you have of meeting men who are really camera buffs. Dress casually but nicely, and go in the evenings or early on a Saturday morning when the store isn't too busy. You want to find someone who can spend the time answering your questions without losing a sale to another customer.

First find a salesman who is not wearing a wedding ring. If all of the salespeople are married (or are women or aren't your type), look around for a while at the other customers. Most people who are looking at camera equipment are willing to talk about photography. If you see an interesting customer, begin to look at equipment in the same general area he's looking in. If he seems very serious, you can ask him if he's a professional photographer and what type of camera he prefers. Tell him you're just starting out yourself and wonder what type of camera he'd recommend.

If you find a salesman who seems like a potential Mr. Right, explain that you are looking for a camera, but have a limited budget. Let the person describe the type of cameras available, but also ask if you should come back at a better time if he seems too busy. Don't buy a camera until you have visited most of the shops in the area. Remember that the process itself is important in bringing you in touch with new men. The electronics department of a department store is another place to research cameras and meet interesting men. Along the way you should be learning a great deal about camera equipment, too.

If your budget is very limited, use the knowledge you've acquired to search the newspaper ads for used camera equipment. You can probably buy an old 35mm camera in good condition for under a hundred dollars. Following up on the ads will also bring you in contact with new people.

Once you've bought your equipment, sign up for a class. If you don't find anyone interesting in your first class, sign up for another. Keep at it. If nothing else, you'll be acquiring the ability to pursue a lifelong hobby. And a camera is one of the most valuable "props" you can have as you look for men.

You can go almost anywhere by yourself if you are carrying a camera and are shooting pictures. You can look through a camera (especially with a telephoto lens) at almost anyone without feeling self-conscious. You can even go up to someone and ask him if you could take his picture. Hardly anyone minds being photographed by a stranger—and you can certainly find a way to start a conversation after photographing someone.

Try going to a sports event by yourself, carrying a camera. Shoot the event as part of your assignment for class. Or give yourself the assignment of shooting pictures of men. Photography classes usually assign you to shoot people as well as places.

Remember that as you are shooting pictures, you are also being watched by people. It is easy for a man to approach you and ask what you're photographing. So while you're looking for subjects to photograph, be sure you smile and look attractive, too.

6. *"Adopt" a Child or an Animal.* Many single women find that owning a dog is more responsibility than they want, but there are lots of families with dogs who would

love to have help in caring for their animal. Befriend someone with a dog and offer to walk him in the morning, after
work, or on weekends. Tie a bright bandanna around the
dog's neck and set off on a walk, smiling at people as you
pass. Having a dog to walk gives you a sense of confidence
and is a great conversation starter.

You might also offer to babysit a friend's child on
weekends or after work. Take the child to the zoo, a museum, or a playground. Go someplace fun where you'll see
lots of other people. Learn to enjoy the world of children.
Laugh. Roll down hills. Throw a frisbee. Giggle. Skip. Eat
ice cream. The more you learn to let go and enjoy yourself
in a childlike way, the more attractive you will be to many
men. You may be surprised by the way a man will feel free
to talk to you when he sees you playing with a child. And
it's easy to say something like, "Isn't he cute? He's my neighbor's boy, but I love playing with him," quickly establishing
your availability.

7. Volunteer. There are so many ways to get involved
in worthy causes. And being a volunteer gives you the opportunity to meet a whole new group of people. As you
look at the many possibilities, consider what other people
would be attracted to the cause. For example, helping in a
women's shelter is a very worthy cause, but you probably
won't meet many single men that way. Consider, instead
involving yourself in a cause sponsored by the Jaycees or
another civic group. Watch for churches that are launching
clean up efforts or working with groups like Habitat for
Humanity. Those efforts attract all types of individuals
who are interested in helping the poor.

Volunteer to help in a political campaign on a local
level. You'll get to know many people while learning more
about the political process. Offer to help at sporting events,
such as golf tournaments. Become a guide at a local museum.
Inquire about the need for volunteers at a local theater. The

ushers are often unpaid workers who love the theater and want to see the presentation free of charge.

Remember to explore all of the possible ways to volunteer through your church. You may be surprised at the opportunities for outreach to your community available through your church. And you're sure to meet people who share your values in the process.

8. Join a Sports or Hobby Club. If you like to ski, join a local group and go on a day trip to a local resort. Or learn to sail through a sailing club. Or perhaps you'd prefer to collect stamps or coins. Almost every city has hobby or sports clubs of some kind. Explore as many as you can. No one cares if you aren't an expert. Most clubs enjoy an enthusiastic newcomer. Remember to use this as a way to meet new people and explore new interests. And, of course, remember that the needlepoint club or gardening club will probably have little appeal to single men.

9. Join a Car Club. Car clubs are full of men who are crazy about their cars. Many clubs have women, too, but the majority of most car club members are men. If you are at all interested in a certain type of car—the more exotic, the better—find out about joining the club. If you don't know much about the car, it's better to go to a car meet or general program sponsored by the club instead of monthly meetings where you're more likely to meet the "hard core" enthusiasts.

Because my husband is fascinated with cars, I've attended several Ferrari meets and shows. I doubt my husband will ever own such a car, but he loves to look at them. No one seems to mind if you actually own a Ferrari or not. It's enough that you are interested enough to show up. And you meet people you'd never meet anywhere else.

Check your telephone directory for the car clubs in your area, or call your local car dealer.

10. *Take Up Painting.* Just the other day I saw an attractive young woman with a portable easel camped out on one of the busiest corners in our city. She was painting a very impressionistic picture of the building across the street (at least I think that's what it was) while people hurried by. I noticed that several people, including men in business suits, stopped long enough to look at her picture, ask what she was painting, or mention that she had some blue paint on her nose. She told me that she was painting the picture for an art class, but I thought it was a brilliant way to meet people. You may want to try it.

11. *Go to a Laundromat.* Even if you have a washer and dryer in your home or apartment, periodically go to the laundromat. Find an area where there are lots of apartments, dress casually, but attractively, carry an interesting book or magazine, and "camp out" on a Saturday morning (when most men do their laundry). Conversation openers are easy: "Do you have a quarter for two dimes and a nickel?" "Are there always so many people here this time of day?" (Like the health club line, it establishes when you'll see him there regularly.) "Do you know if these dryers run very hot?"

Time your clothes to come out of the dryer when his do (you can always run them through for another cycle after they're dry!) and you may wind up getting a cup of coffee or lunch together.

Remember that wearing a t-shirt with a college name or carrying an interesting book is a good way not only to start a conversation, but also to establish something of your values orientation.

12. *Grocery Shop Often.* Most men shop for groceries after work or on weekends. Your chances of meeting someone increases if you shop a few times a week instead of once a week. Sure it's less efficient, but it doesn't cost you any more to buy twelve items one at a time than to buy them all at once. And if you shop after work while you're still dressed up, you'll catch the eye of the single men who are doing the same thing.

Remember that every grocery store has its own type of customer. There is one store near my home that seems to cater to little old women. Another store, only a few blocks away, has a noticeably younger clientele. A store in a singles area of town has been dubbed "the social Safeway" because so many single men and women go there and seem to meet one another. Shop around until you find a store that attracts more people your age. Try different stores.

Be sure to linger over the single-serve frozen meals and other areas where single men seem to congregate. Don't be afraid to ask someone for help in finding something. Most grocery stores are safe places to talk to someone, and even those of us who aren't trying to meet someone naturally strike up conversations with strangers over the melons.

13. *Go to Department Stores Often*. The object of your visit is not to buy a new dress, but to meet a man, either in the men's department or the electronics department. Pick out a tie for your father or brother (there's always an occasion coming up!). Ask the advice of a man who's also looking at the ties.

Go to the electronics department and inspect the new stereos. Or look at the calculators or cameras. Go with the expressed mission of meeting someone. You'll be surprised at how many single men you'll find in evenings or on weekends in an electronics department or a men's department.

14. *Check Out New Cars*. Dress well enough to be taken seriously, then go to a new car showroom and check out the cars. Sports cars are better than station wagons, and Saturdays or after work are the best times to meet single men. If there are many customers, don't waste the salesperson's time. Just say that you're beginning your search for a car and want some general information.

Look at the cars, but also look at the men who are looking at the cars. If you see someone interesting, look at the same car he's inspecting. Ask him if he's owned this type of car before. Ask him if he knows how well the dealer services the car. Tell him you like the color. Car showrooms are easy places to talk to people. Just remember to keep your visit to a reasonably short period of time, don't monopolize the salesperson if you aren't really interested in buying a car (unless you're interested in dating him), and don't ask really basic questions such as, "Is this a good car?"—especially if you are looking at a foreign car or one that appeals to real aficionados.

15. Pursue an Interest in Art. Go to an art museum on a Sunday afternoon all by yourself. Take a guided tour or study a special exhibit. Watch the people who are looking at the paintings. If you see an interesting-looking, single man, position yourself near the next painting or subtly begin to follow him through the exhibit. There's sure to be a painting about which you can say, "How beautiful!" or "Very interesting" or, if all else fails, just lean forward and study the painting with a perplexed look. Then look him in the eye, smile and look slightly confused.

Talking to people in museums is not rude unless you go on and on or do not seem the least bit interested in the subject you are viewing. Neither should you say something terribly critical about a painting (the man might love the style of the painter that you describe as "infantile"). Try going to the museum at different times (remember many museums have seasonal hours) and explore all of the exhibits.

Also become familiar with art galleries in your city, especially ones that display the works of new talents.

Gallery openings are fun and are usually held in the early evening. The style of dress tends toward artsy and interesting or chic and elegant, although there are almost always some people attending in blue jeans (especially the artist). Look interested in the art, but introduce yourself to people. Don't wait for others to introduce themselves to you. I've met some of the most fascinating people at gallery openings. Some have been wealthy collectors; some have been poor friends of the artist. Don't be intimidated by the atmosphere. Be open, sincere, and appreciative, and you're sure to meet new people.

16. Join an Airline Club. Most airlines have wonderful lounges in major airports where frequent fliers relax between flights or while waiting for a plane. The fees to join the clubs vary (see the appendix), but anyone can join, even if they never fly at all.

Most clubs are busiest during the week and are full of businessmen who are just "killing time." Most of the time I spend in these clubs is due to my traveling. But all I have to do is show my membership card to get in. No one cares if I'm actually flying somewhere. Sometimes I use the clubs to meet people who are coming in from out of town. I've even gone to an airline club just to have a quiet place to write.

Most people in the clubs are dressed in business clothes and carry a briefcase, so you should dress appropriately if you want to meet someone. Sit in an area where there is more of a lounge setting, or sit near the TV. There's often a group of people watching a sporting event or the news. In fact, if you don't have anyone to watch Monday night football or the World Series with, head for one of these lounges and you're sure to meet someone.

Since I spend a great many hours in these places, I know that it is not uncommon to be in a club for hours due to a layover or canceled flight. I've met dozens of people this way, especially if I'm reading something that interests them or if we're all waiting out a storm. So don't feel self-conscious if you go into a club. Most people are there by themselves. Get a cup of coffee (all clubs offer free beverages, and some have snacks), sit down, and read a magazine or write a letter. If someone asks you where you're going, say you just came to the club for some peace and quiet. Then ask them where they're going. You'll be involved in a conversation in no time at all.

Maybe this sounds like more trouble than it's worth. But a flight attendant once told me that all of the single attendants tried to get positions in the airline clubs. She said that most of the women working in the clubs were married within a year to men they had met there.

17. Join a Video Club. Some video stores have become a hangout for singles, but there's nothing wrong with meeting someone as you both reach for "Gone With the Wind." You can learn something about a person by the video tapes he selects. But don't go home with someone whom you meet at a video store to watch the movie he's just rented. You can meet people this way, but you will know very little about them after ten minutes in the video store. Still, the fact that you are both checking out "Casablanca" may be enough to know about a man.

18. Take a Singles Vacation. There are singles cruises (see the appendix), singles resorts (such as Club Med), and singles tours. Many colleges offer vacations that are essentially for singles. Some people balk at this, but why not go on a vacation with a group of people whom you know are single? If you don't like anyone, just sit under a tree and read for the rest of the time.

There are specifically Christian singles vacations, and some people have been known to marry after meeting each other this way. Why not explore this outlet? It's better than going on vacation alone and finding yourself surrounded by families.

19. Work at a Conference. If you are interested in a certain type of man, you have a good chance of meeting him at a conference that is on a topic of interest to him. If you are specifically interested in meeting a Christian man, attend a denominational conference or a group such as the National Religious Broadcasters or the Evangelical Press Association (see the appendix for more information). Although some conferences are on weekends, many are held during the week. If you have a regular job, you'll have to plan to take vacation time in order to attend. Maybe this seems like a sacrifice, but when you realize how many men attend these conferences and that they may be exactly the kind of person you're looking for, giving up a few vacation days will seem easy.

Your best chance of meeting people is to volunteer to work at the registration desk of the conference. You'll see almost everyone who attends, learn their name, and find out if there is a spouse registered with him. If you meet an interesting man this way, ask him if there is supposed to be a spouse registration. If he's not married, he may say so. If he doesn't indicate that he's single, say, "Did you leave your wife at home?" or "We have a great program for wives. You'll have to bring her next year." He's sure to indicate his marital status. Since you will probably be wearing a badge, he'll know your name and you will know his from his registration. Then you can find an imaginative way to bump into him during the rest of the conference.

Write to the conference organizers well in advance, explain your skills (you'll probably have to be able to type), and ask if you can work for the conference in exchange for being admitted to the sessions. I don't think it's a good idea to say that you are hoping to meet a man this way!

20. *Write an Article or Research a Paper.* You don't
have to have a contract for a book or an assignment from a
magazine to be writing an article. You don't even have to
be in college in order to be writing a research paper. But if
you choose a topic like "Why Single Men Attend Church
Less Than Single Women" or "What Single Men Like and
Dislike about Their Lives," you're sure to meet men who
will interest you.

I had some official and unofficial research assistants
who helped me gather information for this book. If it makes
you feel better, consider yourself an unofficial contributor
to my next book!

Using a clipboard or a reporter's notebook may help
you feel more official as you ask questions. You may want to
type up a list of questions, too. Then set out for a singles
conference or any large gathering and begin by saying, "I'm
doing research on a topic and need to interview single men.
Are you single and would you be willing to spend five minutes answering some questions?"

Some local magazines and newspapers highlight the
achievements of singles. Perhaps you can become a regular
contributor to the publication. Even if you don't get pub-
lished, you'll meet people and develop the confidence to ask
direct questions.

♥ **Ten Best Props
(Or what to take along on a solo outing)**

1. An interesting, but not too heavy, book.
   C. S. Lewis is a good author if you're looking for a Christian man. Men also tend to
   strike up conversations with women reading business books.

2. A recent copy of *Sports Illustrated*. (Not the
   swimsuit issue, unless you have a figure as
   good as the cover model's.)

3. Today's *Wall Street Journal.*

4. A t-shirt with a school name or fun location. Wear one with the name of a Christian school or organization if you want to narrow the field to Christian men. Don't wear a t-shirt with a cutesy or feminist slogan.

5. A hat or sun visor that has a brand name, resort name, or name of a school.

6. A dog. Tie a bright bandanna around his neck.

7. A camera. Invest in a 35mm camera so people think you are somewhat serious about your pursuit of the perfect picture.

8. A tennis or racquetball racquet. If you have a tennis game in two hours, put on your tennis dress (if you have good legs) and go about your business. Or walk to your game.

9. Fun sunglasses.

10. A crazy button that says nothing political, feminist, or combative.

When You're All Alone on a Saturday Night

Sitting at home is not helping you meet someone. Dress appropriately, put on a big smile, and go:

1. To a health club and work out.

2. To a sports event, carrying your camera.

3. To an electronics store.

4. To a bowling alley.

5. To a coffee shop/bookstore.

6. To a video store.

7. To the airport. Watch the planes, or read a book in the airline club.

8. To a car showroom. (Some are open on Saturday nights.)

9. To a drugstore.

10. To the men's section of a department store.

11. To a well-lit laundromat (in a safe area).

12. Grocery shopping.

13. To McDonald's with a neighbor's child.

14. To hear a special speaker at the library.

15. To a concert at a local church.

CHAPTER TWELVE

Happily Ever After

Three months had passed since Janet and I had begun our "breakfast club," and as we met one Monday morning, Janet dropped her notebook on the table and proclaimed, "I'm ready for graduate school!"

When I asked her if this meant she was getting married, she said, "No. But I'm ready for the next step. I've changed myself and my attitudes. I've met lots of men. I've dated some. But I haven't gotten very far in any relationship. It all feels a bit abstract at this point."

"Janet, you're looking for the right man, which may take awhile," I pointed out. "But maybe we should think again about the three stages of relationships."

Using a piece of paper from Janet's notebook, I drew the following diagram:

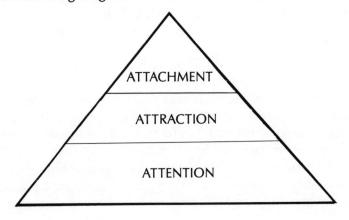

"Most of what we've concentrated on so far has been part of the attention phase," I told Janet. "Maybe we should think about the phases in general terms."

ATTENTION

The attention phase is the very initial phase of a relationship, when a man first notices a woman or a woman notices a man. In this phase, the two people are usually "out of sync"; in other words, one notices the other and begins to be interested, but the other isn't even aware of the interest.

This is certainly the most "shallow" time in a relationship. It is primarily based on physical attraction or proximity. Thus far, we have discussed ways to increase your chances of being noticed by more single men. Volume is important here because you simply aren't going to notice every single man or be noticed by every single man you meet.

Although the attention phase runs counter to the arguments of finding someone with whom you share values, you often have to go through this phase before you find out what the other person values. That's why it's helpful to start out in a place like church where you have some hope of meeting someone who shares your beliefs.

ATTRACTION

The attraction stage occurs when boy notices girl, girl notices boy, and they notice each other noticing. If no one makes a move at this point to further the relationship, it can stall and eventually fall by the wayside.

Getting a guy to ask her out is the first challenge to a woman in this phase of a relationship. This is where all of the "let him know you like him" advice comes in. But what if he does notice and asks you out? It's time to tiptoe through this phase. Here are a few tips to keep in mind.

Go Slowly. If it seems that you've waited forever to hear him ask you out, you may overreact at first. Try to remember that he may be having second thoughts like, "What have I done? What if she thinks I'm a jerk? What if she thinks I'm really crazy about her?" Try to be casually pleased about his invitation. Say something simple like, "I'd really enjoy going out with you. Thanks for calling." That affirms him but doesn't overwhelm him. Don't say, "I thought you'd never ask!" or tell him dramatically, "I'd LOVE to go out with you!"

When you do go out with him, don't tell him your life story in the first hour or make it seem like you are interviewing him for marriage.

Don't Lose Points. You are at risk of losing points more easily than making points with a guy in the early phases of the attraction stage. Most women go out on a first date with the intention of impressing a guy. That's a big mistake. You should go out on the first few dates with the express intention of not losing ground.

Here's what I mean. You can lose points by:

- Dressing inappropriately for the date
- Overdoing hair or makeup
- Not being ready when he picks you up
- Being overly bossy or directive when he asks what you want to do
- Being too shy or uncommunicative
- Talking too much (one of the most common complaints men have)

- Talking too much about your job
- Getting into "dangerous" topics that can divide you (like politics)
- Being opinionated or critical
- Being a gossip
- Ordering the most expensive item on the menu
- Having an awkward time at the end of the date

Just think of your first date or two as a Ping-Pong game. You don't have to do anything clever, you just have to keep the ball in play and return it. Showing off will only make you look foolish.

Focus on Him.   Your chances of making mistakes diminish rapidly when you focus on him. For example, when he asks you out, you might ask him if he's a "blue-jean kind of guy" or if you should wear a dress for your date. If he hasn't told you where you're going or if he's said dinner and a movie, but not told you whether dinner is going to be formal or informal, it's perfectly reasonable to ask him to indicate the appropriate dress.

When you're out on the date, talk about him. Find out what he likes, what's on his mind, what his opinions are. He'll think you're incredibly perceptive if you ask him about his interests. However, be careful to not sound like an interrogator or to ask leading questions like, "So how come a nice guy like you is still single?"

Don't Jump to Conclusions.   Remember that some guys are terribly nervous on a first date, leading them to talk too much, talk too little, seem overly confident, seem overly unconfident, make too few decisions, make too many decisions, etc. Many happily married couples talk about their first dates with wonder that more followed. Give a guy a chance even if he doesn't seem like Prince Charming.

Be Mysterious but Warm. Besides not losing points, you want a guy to be more interested in you and want to get to know you better. The way to accomplish this is to create the air of mystery about you while keeping things focused on him. Unless he's a total egoist, he'll eventually wonder what you think about the topic he's been discussing. Don't say, "I've never really thought about it." Say, "I'm so fascinated to hear your thoughts about this. It makes me want to know more." Or, "I've done some reading on it, but I'm not an expert." Make him work to get to know you.

Cultivate expressions that show you are listening and interested, but aren't telling what you're thinking. Try to develop your own "Mona Lisa" smile. Use your eyes to show him you think he's fascinating.

Be careful not to seem distant while being mysterious. There's a fine line that you can cross if you're not careful. This is where a warm expression will create the right impression.

Tell Him Specific Things about You. When we discussed your personal résumé, we talked about the positive qualities that you needed to emphasize in each phase. During the attraction phase, he is not ready to find out your innermost strengths. He is likely to misread those qualities and think you are getting too serious too fast.

Try to identify three qualities that you want him to understand about you during this stage of the relationship, and let him know about them either directly or by the impression you create.

Qualities you might want to show him include:

- A sense of humor
- Empathy

- Compassion for those less fortunate
- A love of animals
- A love of children (IF you are careful to not sound desperate to have five of your own)
- An interest in sports
- Fascination with current events
- Friendliness

As you can see, these are not deep character qualities, but they do begin to reveal things about you which give him a sense of who you are. Don't be self-deprecating during this stage. You need to show a certain degree of confidence in who you are so that he can feel comfortable with you.

If you've done everything right in the attraction stage, he's thinking, "She's really easy to be with. I want to spend more time with her. I want to get to know her better. She seems to like me, but I may like her more."

You have had the opportunity to get to know him over a few dates, to learn about his interests, hobbies, work, family, and values. Now you can decide if you want to progress to the next stage: attachment.

If you're not sure, you can probably extend the attraction period for a while as you get to know him better. If you're the one who is less sure about where the relationship is going, you may want to try suggesting some different settings for dates in order to see how he reacts under different circumstances. If you feel that he's getting too serious and you don't want to lead him on, you may want to turn him down occasionally when he asks you out so that he gets the hint that he isn't the focus of your life. This is easier than having a serious talk about where the relationship is or isn't going and can help both of you catch your breath before progressing to the next stage.

In my relationship with Bob, we stayed in this phase for nearly six months. I felt that I was too young to get seriously involved; he had recently broken up a four-year-long relationship and didn't want to settle in too quickly again. There were times when this was awkward, yet now I'm grateful that we spent so much time getting to know each other. By the time we progressed to a commitment stage, we felt sure of each other and our emotions.

ATTACHMENT

The attachment stage begins when you are "in sync" and are both clearly interested in deepening the relationship. Some women make the mistake of breathing easily and deciding that they don't have to worry anymore. That's not the case. Men can get very skittish during this stage, wondering how they got so involved or whether they're too young to get serious. Men begin to feel the weight of responsibility at this stage, whereas women begin to relax and decide they're in the home stretch.

Impressions Still Count. It's important to keep an air of courting about this phase so the guy doesn't feel that you're taking him for granted. You might think that the game-playing should be over and you can "be yourself," but he's probably looking at you and wondering what it would be like to spend his life with you. If you begin to look sloppier or treat him less politely, he may pull back, fearing the downhill trend.

Courting should continue even in marriage, so don't feel like you can just let yourself go at any point in the relationship without experiencing a turn in the way he treats you. If you still want him to hold doors open for you or send you flowers, you need to treat him as if he is special too.

I'll never forget a couple I knew in college who seemed to have a wonderfully romantic relationship until they announced their engagement. Soon after, Beth started speaking to Eric as if she were his mother, scolding him, reminding him of his various duties to her, and generally trying to remake him into the man she wanted to marry. This lasted for a year, until the next freshman class entered and a pretty young woman became Eric's lab partner in biology. She obviously worshiped him, and soon he broke off with Beth and married the adoring young woman. Although we sympathized with Beth, few of us were surprised.

Let Him Get to Know You. Don't feel compelled to tell him everything about yourself. But you should feel free to express yourself without fear or hesitation. You should be comfortable enough so that you don't weigh every word or rethink every conversation. If you've progressed to this phase and he isn't really fascinated with you and every detail of your life, he's either totally egotistical or the relationship is really still in the attraction stage and you don't know it.

Don't Have Too Many Expectations. Just because saying "I love you" means you want to spend the rest of your life with him, don't assume it means the same to him. Don't get your hopes up on every holiday that he will "pop the question." At this stage in a relationship, it is easy to believe you know the other person better than you actually do. Surprises are bound to happen. Your relationship has not really stood the test of time or been exposed to enough circumstances to test your assumptions about each other. The more you begin to believe you know him and what he wants, the more you set up the potential for disappointment.

Continue to ask him what he thinks about a variety of issues and become progressively more personal about the topics. Don't assume that he thinks a certain way, ask him.

Go Slowly. This same advice applies equally to both phase two and phase three of the relationship. Most women try to push things along too fast. I do believe there is a point at which you need to ask him to express his intentions or you'll need to move along, but that point probably comes much later than many women assume.

Physical intimacy is another area of confusion to women, especially Christian women who say that they feel caught in the double standard that is sometimes even prevalent in churches. When I interviewed Christian men in their twenties, most expressed a desire to marry a woman who had not been sexually involved with another man. However, they did want to marry a woman with whom they could have an enjoyable sexual relationship after marriage.

Setting the tone for the physical side of the relationship is primarily up to the woman. That doesn't mean that you shouldn't kiss a guy on the first date. But it does mean that if you kiss him passionately on the first date, he is going to expect you to be as expressive or more on the second date. Don't get yourself into a situation that brings physical intimacy into a relationship that isn't emotionally intimate. Some couples use physical intimacy as a way to get to know each other instead of letting it follow an emotional bond. It takes work to get to know about each other's interests, values, hopes, and dreams. But if you really want to marry Mr. Right, you'll take the time to get to know him.

Our discussion of the phases of a relationship was the last breakfast Janet and I had for a while. I took a new job, and we didn't see each other for months. But when I bumped into her unexpectedly one day, she hugged me and squealed, "It worked!"

Janet was dating three different men and having a wonderful time. Although one man was seriously interested, she wasn't sure she was ready to settle down since she was having the time of her life.

As I looked at Janet, I was most impressed by the difference I saw in her face. She looked radiant, confident, and attractive. She exuded an energy that made people want to get to know her. She liked herself and it showed.

I knew that when the time came to settle down with Mr. Right, he would be a man who appreciated Janet for the wonderful person she was. She wouldn't be settling for someone to marry; she would be opening the door on a lifelong partnership.

Congratulations! If you've just finished this book you've shown that you are serious about changing your life. You've picked up some tips, you've learned some new attitudes, you're well prepared to search for Mr. Right. Now you need *to do something.*

Don't make excuses; don't second guess responses. Begin to take a risk or two. You *will* see results, not just in how men act toward you, but also in how you feel about yourself. You will form new habits that will soon become second nature. You will shed all habits that have held you back. And don't be surprised if both men and women say things to you like, "You're looking great," because you *will* look great. And Mr. Right will notice.

APPENDIX

FOR MORE ABOUT MEN . . .

Appleton, William S., M.D. *Fathers and Daughters.* New York: Doubleday & Co., 1981.

Witkin-Lanoil, Georgia. *The Male Stress Syndrome.* New York: New Market Press, 1986.

Druck, Ken. *The Secrets Men Keep.* New York: Doubleday & Co., 1985.

Wright H., Norman. *Understanding the Man in Your Life.* Waco: Word, 1987.

Blitchington, Peter and Evelyn. *Understanding the Male Ego.* Nashville: Thomas Nelson, 1984.

Brothers, Joyce. *What Every Woman Should Know about Men.* New York: Ballantine, 1981.

Johnson, James. *What Every Woman Should Know About a Man.* Grand Rapids: Zondervan, 1981.

CHRISTIAN DATING SERVICES

Christian Singles Exchange
Box 83211
San Diego, CA 92138
619-266-8602

Meet Christian Singles
1-800-323-8113, ext. 390
T.K. Publications (Lutheran)
P.O. Box 1411
Canton, OH 44708

Born Again Singles
P.O. Box 4415
El Monte, CA 91734

Christian Contact Service, International
P.O. Box 1281
Fayetteville, AR 72701

Christian Singles Association
P.O. Box 231
El Toro, CA 92630

Christian Singles International
P.O. Box 637
Brighton, IL 62012

Church of Many Mansions
Christian Singles Outreach
P.O. Box 9020
Van Nuys, CA 91409

CSA Christian Singles
P.O. Box 6065
Santa Barbara, CA 93160

Handicapped Introductions (not necessarily Christian)
P.O. Box 48
Coopersburg, PA 18036

Jews for Jesus Singles
P.O. Box 888
New York, NY 10023

CHURCH DENOMINATIONS AND CHRISTIAN ORGANIZATIONS WHICH HOLD CONFERENCES

National Religious Broadcasters
Morristown, NJ 07960
201–428–5400

National Association of Evangelicals
P.O. Box 28
Wheaton, IL 60189
312–665–0500

Evangelical Press Association
P.O. Box 4550
Overland Park, KS 66204
913–381–2017

American Baptist Church in U.S.A.
Valley Forge, PA 19481

Southern Baptist Convention
460 James Robertson Parkway
Nashville, TN 37209

Baptist General Conference
1233 Central St.
Evanston, IL 60201

The Episcopal Church
815 Second Ave.
New York, NY 10017

Evangelical Free Church of America
1515 East 66th St.
Minneapolis, MN 55423

Lutheran Church in America
231 Madison Ave.
New York, NY 10016

Lutheran Church—Missouri Synod
500 N. Broadway
St. Louis, MO 63102

National Baptist Convention USA, Inc.
915 Spain Street
Baton Rouge, LA 70872

Presbyterian Church in America
P.O. Box 256
Clinton, MS 39056

Presbyterian Church USA
341 Ponce de Leon Ave. NE
Atlanta, GA 30365

Reformed Church in America
475 Riverside Dr.
New York, NY 10027

Reformed Presbyterian Church Evangelical Synod
107 Haedy Rd.
Lookout Mountain, TN 39350

United Methodist Church
475 Riverside Dr.
New York, NY 10027

AIRLINE CLUBS

Admirals Club
American Airlines
P.O. Box 650011
Dallas, TX 75262–0081
Fees: One-year membership, $150; call (800) 433–1790.

Braniff Business Club
P.O. Box 1163
Dallas, TX 75221–9990
Fees: Initiation, $25; one year, $50; call (800) 527–5158 or (800)
    272–6433.

Continental Presidents Club
P.O. Box 4555
Houston, TX 77210–4555
Fees: Initiation, $50; one year, $80; call Member Service Center
    (713) 954–1136.

Delta Crown Room
Delta Air Lines
Crown Room Membership Center
Dept. 857
P.O. Box 20533
Atlanta, GA 30320–2533
Fees: One year, $125; call (800) 323–2323.

Eastern Ionosphere Clubs
720 Fifth Avenue, Suite 701
New York, NY 10019
Fees: Initiation, $50; one year, $80; call (800) 243–CLUB.

Northwest WorldClub
Northwest Airlines WorldClub Service Center
MS C6330
Minneapolis/St. Paul International Airport
St. Paul, MN 55111
Fees: Initiation, $50; one year, $110; call (800) 435–9696.

Clipper Club Administration
Pan American World Airways
200 Park Avenue, Fifth Floor
New York, NY 10166
Fees: Initiation, $25; one year, $150; call (212) 880–1765.

Piedmont Presidential Suite
USAir Club Administration
National Airport
Washington, DC 20001
Fees: One year, $100; call (800) 828–8522.

TWA Ambassadors Club
P.O. Box 223567
Dallas, TX 75222
Fees: One year, $150; call (800) 527–1468.

United Airlines Red Carpet Club
Pick up applications at airports, travel agents.
Fees: Initiation, $100; one year, $85.

TRAVEL IDEAS FOR SINGLES

Travel Companion Exchange (not necesssarily Christian)
P.O. Box 833
Amityville, NY 11701

Christian Cruises for Singles:

Found Free Travel Club (emphasis on contemporary
        Christian music)
P.O. Box 7988
Fremont, CA 94537
415-792-3442

Clergy Travel Agency
2300 Henderson Mill Road
Suite 325
Atlanta, GA 30345
800-458-8281

New Creation Worldwide Cruises
P.O. Box 14837
Orlando, FL 32857
800-554-5454

Christian Cruise Conferences
2220 Tulare St.
Fresno, CA 93721